Everything That ... in the Kitch...

A Glamper's Guide to Camp Cooking

Simple, Healthy, Delicious Meals

by Dianne Linderman

Illustrated by Delores Uselman Johnson & Alexandra Linderman

A Glamper's Guide to Camp Cooking

Published by Dianne Linderman
Printed in the United States of America

For information, contact:
Dianne@EverythingThatMattersRadio.com

www.EverythingThatMattersInTheKitchen.com
https://www.youtube.com/user/diannelinderman1

ISBN-13: 978-1546521235
ISBN-10: 1546521232

Cover Art by Alexandra Linderman
Cover Design by Connie Walser Derek
Interior Art by Mila Designs, Dolores Uselman Johnson and Alexandra Linderman

Dedicated to my children,
Luke & Alexandra,
my husband, David,
my Mom & Dad,
my 4 brothers and their wives,
my 17 nieces and nephews
and grand nephew.

Who wants to go Glamping?

The answer is:

Everyone who loves a little romance and a lot of atmosphere with a touch of glamour! When it first caught on, Glamping was usually a group of ladies getting together with their vintage trailers for a few days of camping; sharing food and striving to have the cutest setup. They would bring a little wine and were always competing to make the best Glamping recipes.

But lately families have been getting in on the act. Glamping can be as simple as a campsite that you set up with a few extra touches, like an adorable tablecloth and even some romantic lighting. I always have really nice camp chairs and even an outdoor rug next to the fire and a couple of hammocks. Or you can do it up, with a chandelier hanging in a tree, music and nice dishes. I even know someone who brought a claw-foot bathtub to the Glamp site.

I am an all-American vintage lady, and I like everything that has charm and a touch of the 40s and 50s. One of my favorite looks is 1950s with a lot of red and white gingham or plaid wool blankets, or even as simple as some pastel pinks with a vintage flare.

Life is an adventure, and everywhere I go I get ideas for simple, healthy cooking. My favorite way to cook is one-pot meals. Inside this book you will find the beginning of my collection of recipes that are so simple and unbelievably delicious that you can use them when you go Glamping or camping or at home in your own kitchen!

Don't let life get you down; find the beach, the mountains or drive to the forest, and create a little movie set. Bring your kids, family and friends. These will be the best memories you will ever experience.

Enjoy and keep it simple!

Dianne Linderman

Momma's
GOOD
FOOD
GOOD
FOOD

Contents

Fishing
Hiking
Campground

Eggs, Breakfast & More

Deviled Eggs

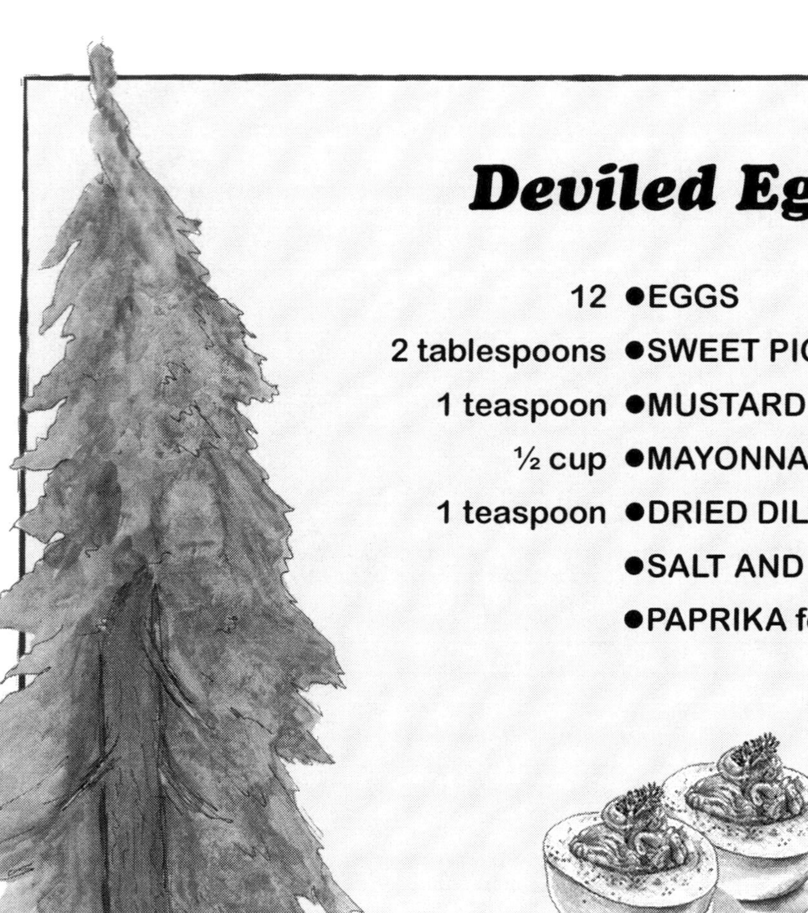

12	●EGGS
2 tablespoons	●SWEET PICKLE RELISH
1 teaspoon	●MUSTARD
½ cup	●MAYONNAISE OR VEGANIASE
1 teaspoon	●DRIED DILL WEED
	●SALT AND PEPPER to taste
	●PAPRIKA for sprinkling on top

Boil Eggs. Cool or chill them, then peel and cut in half.

In a mixing bowl, place all of the yolkes and all of the ingredients, except paprika. Mix well with a mixer until creamy.

Spoon into egg white halves, and place on a pretty plate. Sprinkle with paprika then chill.

Yum!

French Toast

1	●EGG per piece of toast
1 tablespoon per egg	●HEAVY CREAM
4 slices	●BREAD (Milton's Healthy Whole Wheat)
½ teaspoon	●VANILLA
¼ teaspoon	●CINNAMON (optional)
3 tablespoons	●COCONUT OIL, organic — will not burn!
	●PURE MAPLE SYRUP
	● FRESH BERRIES & WHIPPED CREAM

Beat eggs, cream, cinnamon, and vanilla together in a shallow bowl.

Dip each slice of bread into the egg mixture, allowing bread to soak up some of the mixture.

Place coconut oil in a large skillet on medium high heat. Add as many slices of bread onto the skillet as will fit at a time. Fry until brown on both sides, flipping the bread when necessary.

Serve hot with butter, maple syrup, and if available, fresh berries and whipped cream.

Hash Brown Potato Pancakes

1 bag organic	●HASH BROWN POTATOES
3	●EGGS
2 tablespoons	●OAT FLOUR
1 tablespoon	●MAYONNAISE or VEGENAISE
	●GARLIC SALT & PEPPER to taste
½	●ONION, minced
3 to 4 tablespoons	●COCONUT OIL, for frying

Pre-heat coconut oil in a large fry pan with the heat on high.

In a bowl, stir all ingredients together; make sure the hash browns are not frozen. If you need your mixture to be a little stiffer, add more oat flour.

Form patties with your hands, then gently lay them into the hot coconut oil. Turn heat down to medium and fry well on one side before turning. Make sure you brown the patties well on both sides. Sprinkle with garlic salt and pepper.

Yum!

Pumpkin Pancakes

1 cup	●WHOLE WHEAT FLOUR
1 cup	●OAT FLOUR
2 tablespoons	●COCONUT SUGAR (or use a stevia baking blend)
2 ½ teaspoons	●BAKING POWDER
½ teaspoon	●SALT
1 teaspoon	●CINNAMON
½ teaspoon	●ALLSPICE
½ teaspoon	●GINGER
2 cups	●NONFAT MILK
1 teaspoon	●VANILLA
3 tablespoons or more	●COCONUT OIL
1 cup	●CANNED PUMPKIN

For Glamping: Make dry mixture ahead of time and store in a plastic bag.

Mix all the dry ingredients together in a bowl.

Mix all the wet ingredients in with the dry ingredients until there are no clumps.

Use coconut oil and cook on medium heat until the edges look dry, then flip. These pancakes are supposed to be dense and thick.

Serve with REAL MAPLE SYRUP.

Ultimate

Breakfast Burrito

Large	●TORTILLA, low carb or whole wheat
2 per person	●EGGS, scrambled
½	●ONION, sautéed
	●SPINACH or other VEGGIES, sautéed
Any type	●MEAT, CHICKEN or FISH
	●CHEESE of your choice, shredded
	●BLACK BEANS, refried or whole
	●VEGGIES
	●SALSA

This is where you can get creative if you have left-over meat, chicken, fish or veggies. A low-carb tortilla makes a great breakfast, lunch, or dinner burrito.

Place tortilla on paper plate, add all of the ingredients, and fold like a burrito.

In a grill pan, cook both sides. Serve with salsa.

For a lunch or dinner burrito use any meat, chicken or fish. You can use left-overs or a store-bought rotisserie chicken. Then add all the goodies of your choice...black beans, cilantro, tomatoes, cheese, veggies, salsa... be creative!

My notes...

My notes...

Soups

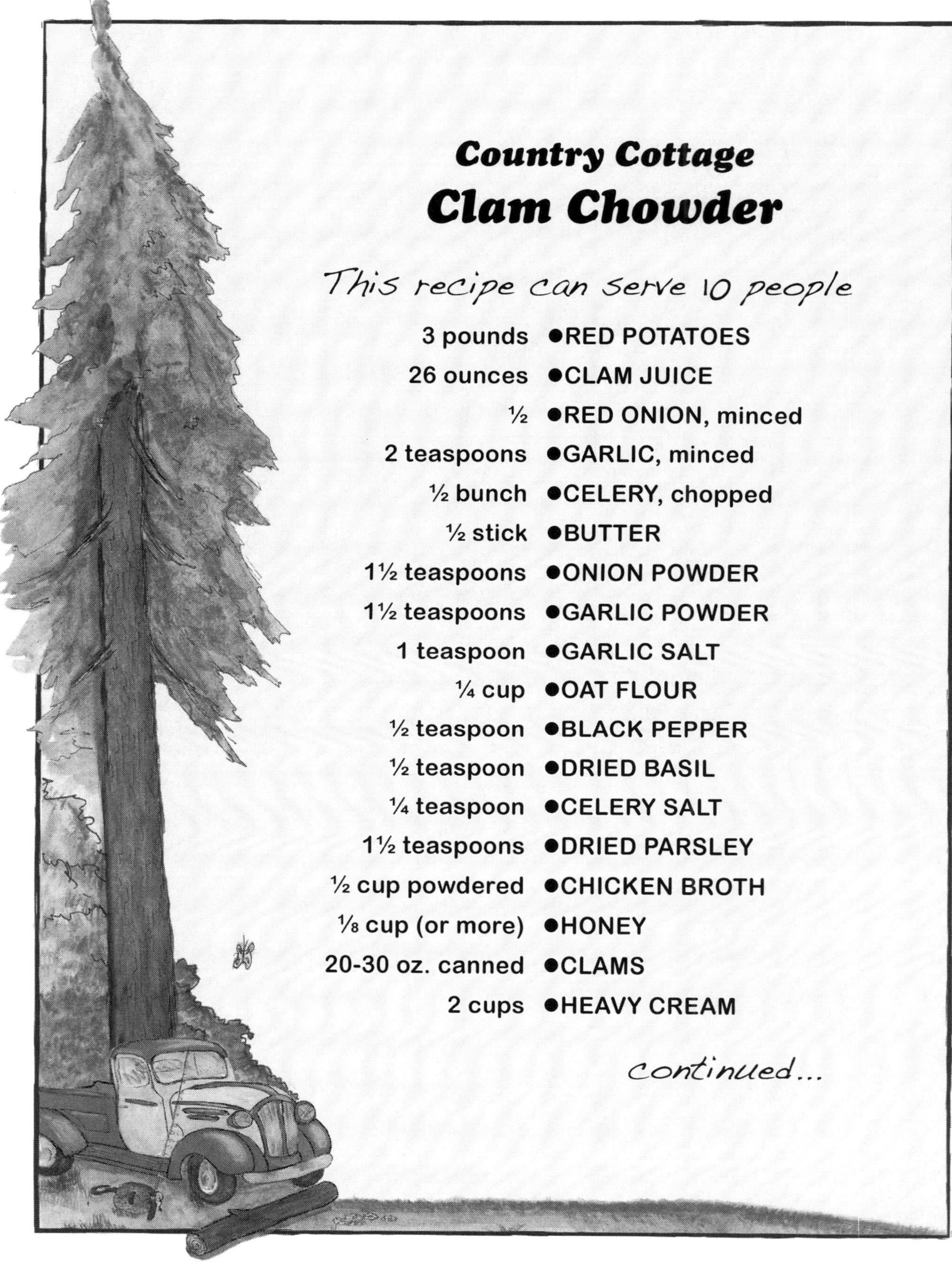

Country Cottage
Clam Chowder

This recipe can serve 10 people

3 pounds	•RED POTATOES
26 ounces	•CLAM JUICE
½	•RED ONION, minced
2 teaspoons	•GARLIC, minced
½ bunch	•CELERY, chopped
½ stick	•BUTTER
1½ teaspoons	•ONION POWDER
1½ teaspoons	•GARLIC POWDER
1 teaspoon	•GARLIC SALT
¼ cup	•OAT FLOUR
½ teaspoon	•BLACK PEPPER
½ teaspoon	•DRIED BASIL
¼ teaspoon	•CELERY SALT
1½ teaspoons	•DRIED PARSLEY
½ cup powdered	•CHICKEN BROTH
⅛ cup (or more)	•HONEY
20-30 oz. canned	•CLAMS
2 cups	•HEAVY CREAM

continued...

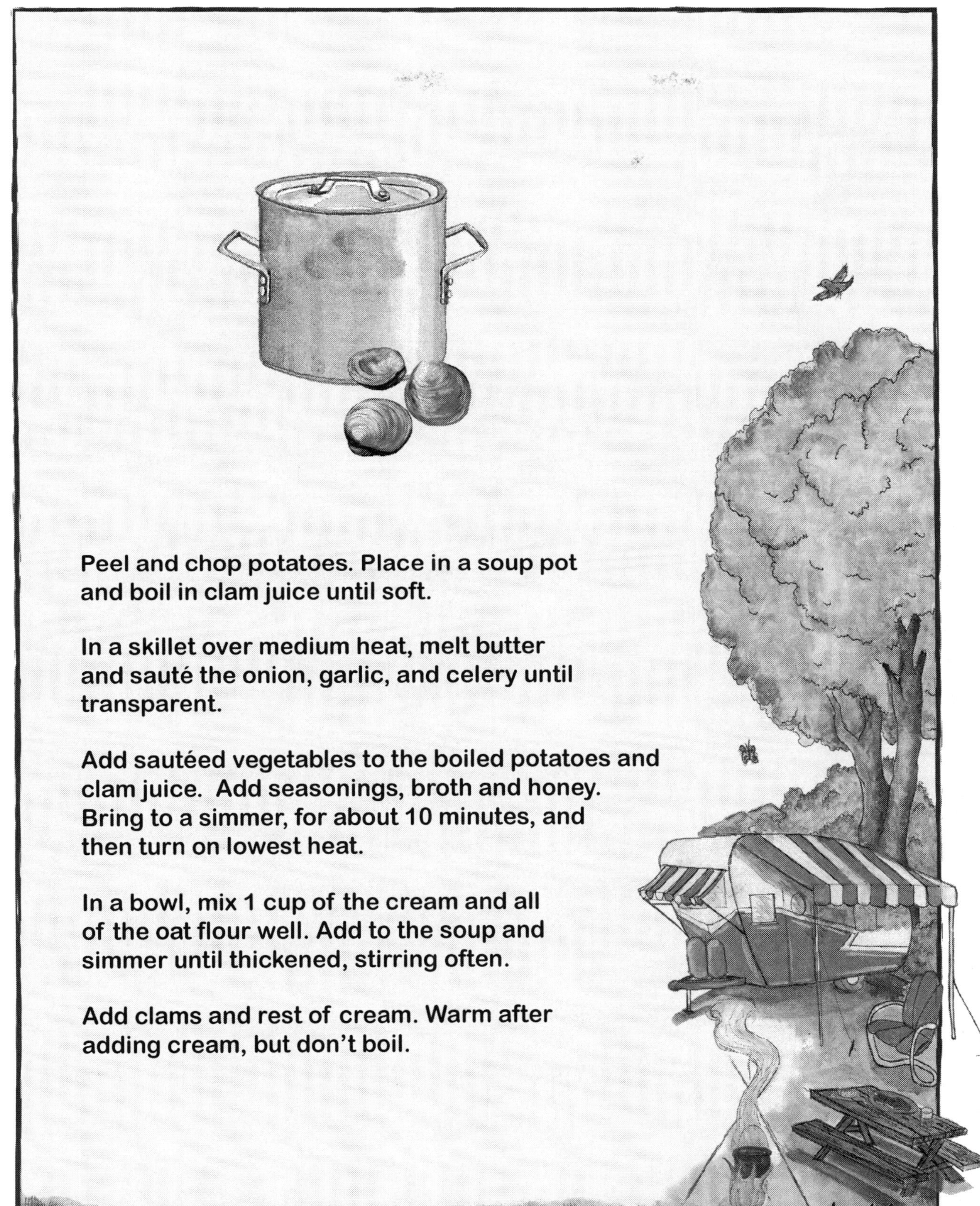

Peel and chop potatoes. Place in a soup pot and boil in clam juice until soft.

In a skillet over medium heat, melt butter and sauté the onion, garlic, and celery until transparent.

Add sautéed vegetables to the boiled potatoes and clam juice. Add seasonings, broth and honey. Bring to a simmer, for about 10 minutes, and then turn on lowest heat.

In a bowl, mix 1 cup of the cream and all of the oat flour well. Add to the soup and simmer until thickened, stirring often.

Add clams and rest of cream. Warm after adding cream, but don't boil.

Creole Jambalaya

2 tablespoons	●BUTTER or COCONUT OIL
1 large	●SWEET ONION, chopped
8	●GREEN ONIONS, chopped
2	●CELERY RIBS, chopped
3 cups (1 lb.)	●COOKED HAM, cubed (organic or non-nitrate ham)
1 pound	●Cajun or SMOKED SAUSAGE, sliced
1 8-oz can	●TOMATO SAUCE
	●GARLIC SALT to taste
	●PEPPER to taste
¼ ground	●RED PEPPER
2 cups tiny	●SHRIMP
5 cups	●BROWN RICE, uncooked

Melt butter in a large skillet.

Add onions and celery; sauté until tender.

Add ham, sausage and the next 4 ingredients. Cook for 20 minutes while stirring.

Stir in rice. Cover and cook, stirring occasionally, on low heat for 30 minutes.

Before serving, add shrimp and stir to mix.

Smoked Salmon Chowder

4 tablespoons ●BUTTER
½ cup ●ONION, chopped
2 stalks ●CELERY, chopped
¼ ●WHITE WINE
5 cups ●CHICKEN BROTH—or for best results use CLAM JUICE
1 ●BAY LEAF
3 ●POTATOES, chopped
7 oz. ●SALMON, cooked, de-boned
●GARLIC SALT & PEPPER to taste
1½ cups ●CREAM
2 teaspoons ●Liquid Smoke (optional)
● FRESH DILL & CHIVES

Melt butter in a sauce pan. Add chopped onions, celery and sauté them until translucent. Add the wine to deglaze the pan and get all those yummy browned bits up in the mix.

Fill a soup pot with the broth. Add bay leaf, sautéed vegetables and chopped potatoes. Bring to a boil for 15 minuets, and then turn on low.

Add cooked, de-boned salmon, liquid smoke, cream, and garlic salt and pepper to taste.

Garnish with fresh dill and chives.

Gumbo

4 to 6 pieces	•CHICKEN, dark or light
	•GARLIC SALT & PEPPER, to taste
¼ cup	•OLIVE, or COCONUT OIL
1 pound	•SMOKED SAUSAGE, Nitrate-free, ¼ slices
¼ cup	•OAT FLOUR
5 tablespoons	•BUTTER
1 large	•SWEET ONION, chopped
8 cloves	•GARLIC, minced
1	•GREEN BELL PEPPER, seeded and chopped
3 stalks	•CELERY, chopped
¼ cup	•WORCESTERSHIRE SAUCE
¼ bunch	•FLAT LEAF PARSLEY, coarsely chopped
4 cups	•CHICKEN BROTH
1 14-ounce can	•STEWED TOMATOES with juice
2 cups frozen	•OKRA, sliced
4	•GREEN ONIONS, white and green parts, sliced
½ pound	•SMALL SHRIMP, peeled, deveined and cooked
6 cups	•BROWN RICE cooked in Chicken Broth

continued...

Season the chicken with garlic salt and pepper.

Heat the oil in a heavy bottomed Dutch oven over medium-high heat. Cook the chicken until browned on both sides and remove.

Add the sausage, cut into ¼-inch slices, and cook until browned, then remove.

Make a roux: Sprinkle the flour over the oil. Add 2 tablespoons of butter and cook over medium heat, stirring constantly, until brown—about 10 minutes. Let it cool.

Return the Dutch oven to low heat and melt the remaining 3 tablespoons of butter. Add the onion, garlic, green pepper and celery and cook for 10 minutes.

Add Worcestershire sauce, salt and pepper to taste, and the 1/4 bunch parsley. Cook, while stirring frequently, for 10 minutes.

Add 4 cups hot beef broth, whisking constantly.

Add the chicken and sausage. Bring to a boil, then reduce the heat, cover, and simmer for 45 minutes.

Add tomatoes and okra. Cover and simmer for 1 hour.

Just before serving add the green onions, shrimp and parsley.

Serve over brown rice.

Sweet Potato & Fish Soup

12 ounce ●WHITE FISH FILLET, skinned
Scant 1 cup ●SWEET POTATO, diced
1 ●ONION, chopped
2 ●CARROTS, diced
7½ cups ●VEGETABLE STOCK
14 ounces ●CLAMS with CLAM JUICE
1 cup ●DRY WHITE WINE
1 cup ●LIGHT CREAM
●GARLIC SALT & PEPPER to taste
Fresh ●PARSLEY for garnish, chopped

Put the fish, sweet potato, onion and carrots into a pan, pour in 4 cups of vegetable stock, and bring to a boil. Reduce the heat, cover, and simmer for 30 minutes.

Meanwhile make sure clams are clean, removing any broken shells. Place clams into a pan with wine, cover and cook over high heat.

Remove the pan of fish and vegetables from the heat and let cool slightly, then ladle the mixture into a food processor or blender in batches and process until smooth.

Return blended soup back to pot, add the remaining wine and clam broth and bring to a boil. Reduce the head and gradually stir in the cream: do not let the soup boil.

Add clams and season to taste with salt and pepper. Heat well and serve immediately.

Garnish with parsley and a drizzle of olive oil.

Scallop Chowder

4 teaspoons	●BUTTER
1½ cups	●ONION, chopped
¼ cup	●CELERY, chopped
3 teaspoons	●GARLIC, minced
4½ cups	●RED POTATOES, unpeeled and chopped
1½ teaspoons	●GARLIC SALT
1 teaspoon ground	●BLACK PEPPER
1/½ teaspoons fresh	●THYME, chopped
6 cups	●CLAM JUICE
¼ cup	●OAT FLOUR for thickening
1½ cups	●MILK
1½ cups	●HALF & HALF
1½ pounds	●SEA SCALLOPS, cut into 1-inch chunks
¼ cup fresh	●CHIVES, chopped

In a sauce pan, sauté onions, celery and garlic in butter over medium heat.

Pour clam juice into a large soup pot and add all veggies, potatoes, herbs, spices, salt and pepper. Bring to a simmer and simmer until potatoes fall apart.

Add flour, stirring well with whisk, and continue to simmer until the soup begins to thicken.

Add everything else. Scallops cook very fast, and cream should not be boiled. This is as good as clam chowder!

Creamy Cauliflower Soup

2	●CAULIFLOWER heads, chopped
1	●MAUI SWEET ONION, chopped
2 stalks	●CELERY, chopped
1 cup	●PARSLEY, minced
4 to 6 cups	●CHICKEN BROTH, or enough to barely cover cauliflower
2	●GARLIC CLOVES, minced
1 cup	●HEAVY CREAM
1 cup or more	●CHEDDAR CHEESE, shredded
	●GARLIC SALT & PEPPER, to taste

In a large pot over medium heat, simmer cauliflower, onion, garlic, celery and parsley in chicken broth until soft.

Blend in a blender being careful not to put too much hot soup in the blender. You can blend half of the soup if you like chunky soup. If you are camping, use a whisk till blended to your liking.

Add the cream, cheese, salt, and pepper to taste.

Don't over heat the soup once cream and cheese are added.

This is a delicious soup and will stick to your ribs. It is very low in carbs.

Cream of Potato Soup

3 lbs. organic	●RED POTATOES, washed and quartered
1 whole	●SWEET ONION, chopped
1 bunch	●FRESH PARSLEY, minced
3 stalks	●CELERY
2 cloves	●GARLIC, minced
5 pieces	●BACON, cooked and chopped
	●CHICKEN BROTH (2 boxes), or make your own—enough just to cover all ingredients.
	●GARLIC SALT & PEPPER to taste
2 teaspoons	●MAPLE SYRUP (optional)
⅛ cup	●CREAM
1 cup or more	●CHEDDAR CHEESE

In large soup pot place onion, garlic, parsley, celery, potatoes and bacon.

Barely cover these ingredients with organic chicken broth and simmer on medium until potatoes are falling apart.

Use whisk or potato masher to puree soup. If you have electricity, use a hand blender.

Yummy!

Tomato Basil Soup

- 6 to 8 large vine-ripened ● TOMATOES, organic
- 1 cup ● BASIL, fresh
- 1 cup ● WHOLE CREAM or MILK, optional
- 2 cups ● CHICKEN BROTH
- 3 to 4 cloves ● GARLIC, fresh, diced
- ● GARLIC SALT & PEPPER to taste
- ⅛ cup ● WHITE WINE (optional)
- 1 to 3 tablespoons ● MAPLE SYRUP, unless tomatoes are really sweet
- ● TABASCO or other HOT SAUCE (if you like spicy soup)

Men, this soup is great for your prostate!

Purée all ingredients in a blender. If you want chunky soup, blend half of the soup a little less.

Warm, don't cook this soup for optimum health. If you like a richer soup, you can add ⅛ cup of white wine and simmer on low.

Don't be afraid to experiment and add ingredients like Parmesan cheese. Garnish with some fresh basil.

Note: If you are glamping/camping use a wisk to blend soup—it works great!

Real Jewish

Chicken Noodle Soup

1 large whole	●CHICKEN, rinsed
3 large	●CARROTS, chopped
3 stalks	●CELERY, chopped into large pieces
1 Maui	●SWEET ONION, chopped
1 whole bunch	●PARSLEY, finely chopped
2 cloves	●GARLIC, minced (optional)
	●SALT & PEPPER to taste
2 cups pre-cooked	●NOODLES or RICE (brown rice is delicious!)

In a large soup pot, combine all the ingredients with the exception of the noodles/rice. Add enough water to cover all ingredients. Cover pot with a lid and simmer over medium heat for approximately 1 hour and 15 minutes.

Cook noodles or rice separately.

Allow to cool slightly. Skim soup of all visible fat, return to stove and warm on medium heat.

To Serve: Place noodles or rice and chicken pieces into individual bowls. Ladle hot soup over it and serve immediately.

A bowl of this soup can do wonders to soothe your cold symptoms!

My notes...

Sandwiches, Pizza & Wraps

Avocado Sandwich

2 Slices ●WHOLE GRAIN BREAD
●MAYONNAISE or VEGENAISE
●LETTUCE and/or SPROUTS
●CUCUMBER
●PICKLE
●TOMATO
●AVOCADO
●LEMON
●SALT & PEPPER
●CHEESE of your choice

Spread mayo on one slice of bread and layer veggies. Squeeze a little lemon and salt and pepper to taste.

On the other slice of bread, place your favorite cheese, and melt under broiler. Place on top of bread with veggies.

Yum!

Tomato Basil Baguette

Easy & delicious!

Fresh ●SOURDOUGH or FRENCH BAGUETTE
Laughing Cow ●LOW-FAT CHEESE
●TOMATOES, sliced
Fresh ●BASIL LEAVES
●BALSAMIC VINEGAR
●GARLIC SALT & PEPPER

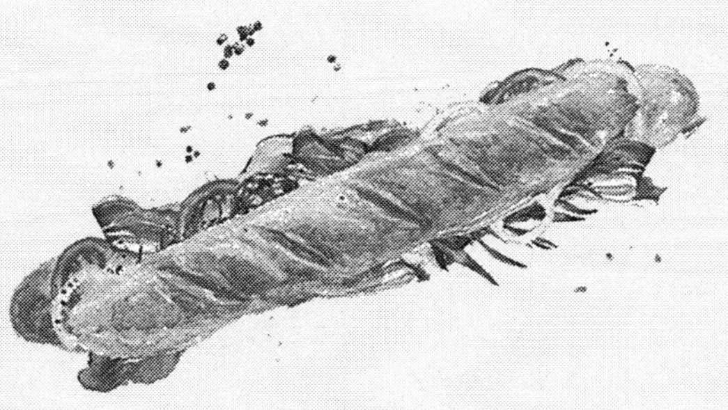

Slice baguette lengthwise down the middle and lay flat.

Spread cheese generously on both sides of the bread.

Place sliced ripe tomatoes on one side of the bread and basil on the other.

Drizzle tomato slices with balsamic vinegar and sprinkle with garlic salt and pepper to taste.

Yum! Yum! Yum!!

Decadent
Grilled Cheese & Tomato Sandwich

2 slices quality organic
- WHOLE WHEAT or OAT BREAD
- MAYONNAISE or VEGENAISE
- CHEESE of your choice; my favorite cheese is white cheddar.
- TOMATO, optional
- BASIL, optional
- BUTTER

Lightly toast two slices of bread.

Spread mayonnaise on both slices.

Lay the cheese, tomato and basil... or whatever you would like, on one slice of bread. Cover with the other slice.

Melt some love (butter) in a pan on the lowest temperature.

Place your sandwich in the melted butter and leave it alone until golden brown, then turn and brown the other side. You also want to make sure the cheese is melted.

Incredible

Egg Salad Sandwich

- 8 large ●HARD BOILED EGGS, chopped
- 3 stalks ●CELERY, finely chopped
- ¼ cup ●MAYONNAISE or VEGENAISE
- 1 whole ●SWEET ONION, chopped
- 2 teaspoons ●YELLOW MUSTARD
- 1 tablespoon ●SWEET PICKLE RELISH
- ●SALT & PEPPER to taste
- Hearty ●WHOLE WHEAT BREAD

Mix all ingredients well.

Heap large spoonfuls onto the bread and serve.

Yum!

Chicken Salad Sandwich

4 to 6 cups	●COOKED CHICKEN, chopped
½ cup	●VEGENAISE MAYO
½ cup	●PINK LADY APPLE, chopped into tiny cubes
¼ cup	●CELERY, chopped
⅛ cup	●FRESH PARSLEY, chopped
½ cup	●SWEET ONION, chopped
2 tablespoons	●YELLOW MUSTARD

Mix well and place on a slice of hearty whole wheat bread, grilled or cold. You can also add lettuce and sliced tomato.

Turkey Pepperoncini Sandwich

Organic	●SOURDOUGH BREAD, sliced
	●MAYONNAISE or VEGENAISE
Nitrate-free	●SMOKED TURKEY, sliced
	●MONTEREY JACK CHEESE, sliced
	●RED ONION, sliced
Handful	●PEPPERONCINIS, sliced
	●TOMATO, sliced
	●SALT & PEPPER
	●RANCH DRESSING

Toast bread until golden brown.

Spread mayonnaise on both slices of bread.

Place turkey on one slice of bread. On other slice, place cheese, red onions and pepperoncini.

Place both sides of sandwich under broiler until cheese is melted.

Add tomato slices, salt and pepper and ranch dressing.

Cut in half and enjoy!

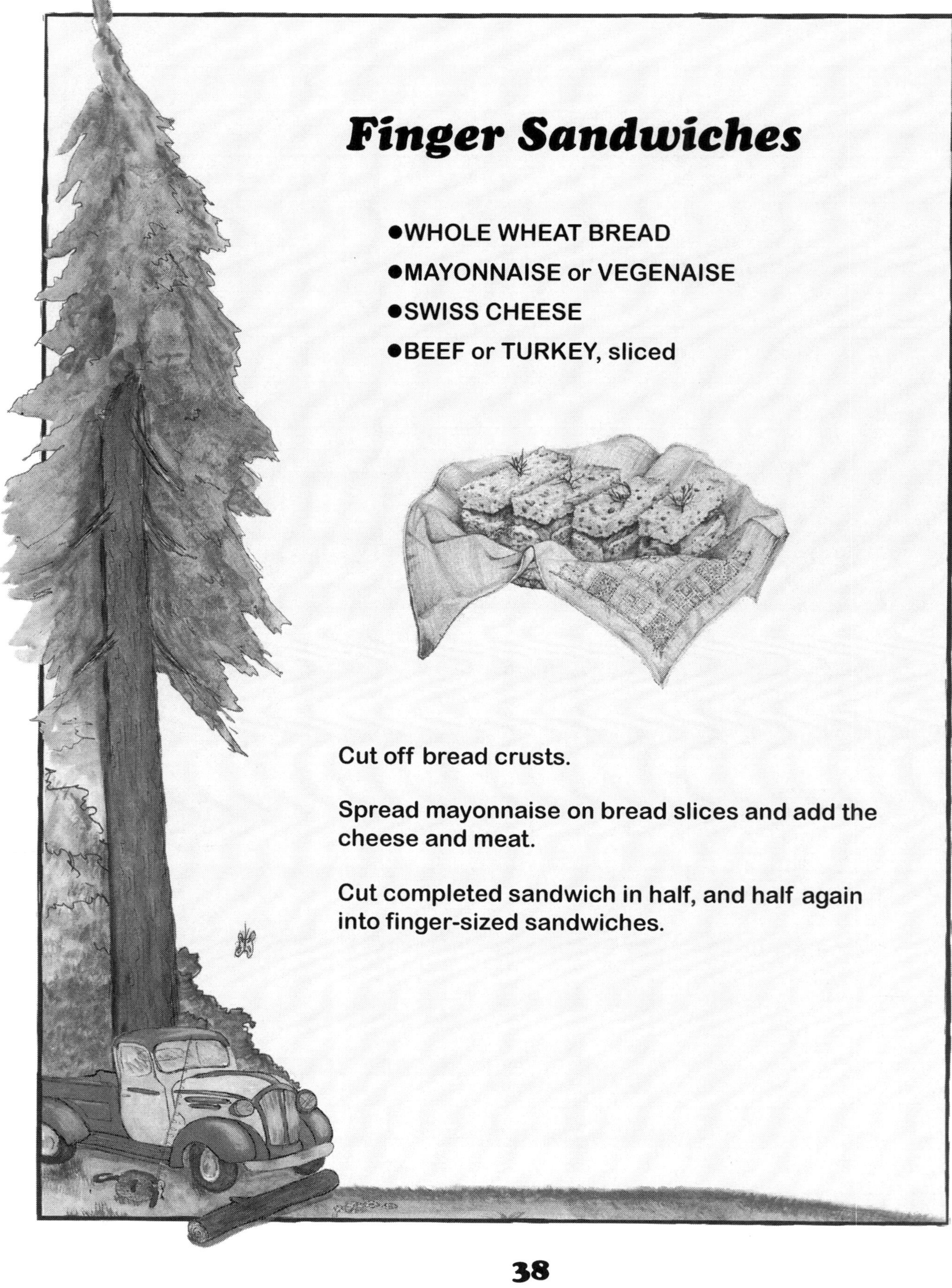

Finger Sandwiches

- WHOLE WHEAT BREAD
- MAYONNAISE or VEGENAISE
- SWISS CHEESE
- BEEF or TURKEY, sliced

Cut off bread crusts.

Spread mayonnaise on bread slices and add the cheese and meat.

Cut completed sandwich in half, and half again into finger-sized sandwiches.

Best Tuna Sandwich

What makes the best tuna sandwich?

#1 Quality BREAD

#2 Quality MAYONNAISE or VEGENAISE

#3 Quality TUNA (in water)

2 cans	●TUNA (squeeze out water)
½ cup	●RED ONION, chopped
⅛ cup (or less)	●SWEET PICKLE RELISH
3 to 5 tablespoons	●MAYONNAISE or VEGENAISE
1 teaspoon	●YELLOW MUSTARD
100%	●WHOLE WHEAT BREAD

Optional

●APPLE, chopped

●TOASTED ALMONDS, chopped

Mix first five ingredients well with fork.

Toast bread (optional), and spread tuna mixture on bread.

Add lettuce, sliced tomato and red onion to your sandwich.

BLTA Sandwich
Bacon, Lettuce, Tomato & Avocado

12 slices Applewood	●SMOKED BACON (no nitrates)
8 pieces of good hearty	●WHOLE WHEAT BREAD
3 to 5 tablespoons	●MAYONNAISE or VEGENAISE
2 small	●AVOCADOS, sliced
8	●TOMATO slices
4 large leaves	●ROMAINE LETTUCE
	●CHEESE, optional
	●SALT & PEPPER to taste

Cook bacon until crisp.

Toast bread.

Spread mayo over both slices.

Layer lettuce on the bottom, next tomatoes, avocados, and lastly the bacon.

Salt and pepper to taste, and place remaining slice of toast on top.

You can cut this into quarters, or cut them in half. Serve with a hearty bowl of soup, or a large salad. Yum!

French Dip Sandwich

Your favorite	●BAGUETTE or FRENCH ROLL
1 to 2 pounds nitrate-free	●ROAST BEEF, sliced
	●MAYONNAISE or VEGENAISE
2 slices	●JACK CHEESE, optional
	●"BETTER THAN BULLION" A JUS

Slice the bread down the middle and grill under a broiler until light brown.

Heat the meat up in a pan.

Spread mayo on both sides of bread.

On one side of bread place a nice pile of meat, and on the other side place the slices of cheese.

Place it back under the broiler and melt the cheese. You may also want to sprinkle the meat with garlic salt.

Meanwhile heat up a cup of a jus.

Slice the sandwich into several pieces so that it can be dipped into the broth.

Yum!

Grilled Pizza

CRUST

Use pre-prepared dough, or...

1 teaspoon	●MAPLE SYRUP
2 packets	●ACTIVE DRY YEAST
2 teaspoons	●OLIVE OIL, plus extra for coating bowl
	●SALT & PEPPER
2 ½ cups	●WHOLE WHEAT PASTRY FLOUR

TOPPINGS

I like use NEWMAN'S TOMATO BASIL MARINARA SAUCE and quality MOZZARELLA CHEESE and then top with fresh TOMATO and BASIL after grilling. You can add any type of VEGGIES or COOKED MEATS, or even make it a taco pizza. Be creative and have fun!

continued...

Combine syrup and yeast in a bowl with 1 cup of warm water and let stand until foamy. Add rest of crust ingredients and mix well.

Turn onto a floured board and knead until dough feels soft.

Place the dough inside a large bowl that has been coated with olive oil and let it stand until it doubles in size. Punch it down and knead it once more on a floured board. Place it back in the bowl and let rise again.

Heat the BBQ grill.

Place the dough back on the floured board and cut it into four sections.

With a floured rolling pin, roll out a section of dough into a round crust.

Brush one side of the dough with oil.

Lay the dough round on the BBQ grill, olive-oil-brushed-side down. Brush the top of the dough with a thin layer of olive oil, too. Let the dough cook for about 3 minutes, with the lid on.

Remove pizza crust from grill and spread with a thin layer of sauce, then add cheese and top with your favorite ingredients—anything goes!

Place loaded pizza back on grill with tin foil on top. Close lid and let bake for approximately 3 to 5 minutes. Keep an eye on the pizza and don 't let it burn; you will know when it's done.

BBQ Pulled Beef Sandwich

3-5 pounds of good quality ●TRI-TIP BEEF
Your favorite ●BBQ SAUCE
●SOURDOUGH ROLLS
●GARLIC SALT
●PEPPER

Cut tri-tip in strips and place in a crock pot. Add a medium-size bottle of BBQ sauce, and garlic salt and pepper to taste.

Turn crock pot on high for 6 hours, or slow cook for 8 hours. If you are camping, cook for 4 hours on medium heat.

When it is done, pull apart the meat and place on large sourdough rolls.

My notes...

My notes...

Tacos, Enchiladas & More

Best Homemade

Homemade Guacamole

3	●AVOCADOS, halved and pitted
1 tablespoon	●LIME JUICE
½ cup	●GREEK YOGURT
	●SALT & PEPPER to taste

In a small bowl, mash avocados with a fork; stir in lime juice, and Greek yogurt.

Mash for a smooth consistency, salt and pepper to taste.

Best Ever
Raw Salsa

½ cup	●SWEET ONION, chopped
¼ cup	●GREEN ONIONS, chopped
1 tablespoon	●CILANTRO, chopped
1 bunch	●Parsley, chopped
1	●JALAPENO PEPPER (or milder pepper) seeded, chopped
3 handfuls	●RED TOMATOES, chopped
1 clove	●GARLIC, peeled
2 to 3	●LIMES, juiced
1 teaspoon	●MAPLE SYRUP
	●SALT to taste

Place all of the ingredients in a food processer and carefully blend with intermittent pulsing and pushing ingredients down until you get to the consistency you like.

Fish Tacos

2 pounds mild	●WHITE FISH or SALMON
2 cups	●RED CABBAGE, shredded
¼ cup	●CILANTRO, coarsely chopped
¼ cup plus 3 tablespoons	●RED SALSA
	● SALT to taste
1 package	●CORN TORTILLAS (large)
	● COCONUT OIL for frying

Fry or bake the fish.

Fry tortillas in coconut oil.

Place cooked fish into tortillas and top off with cabbage, cilantro, and salsa. Add tomatoes—or whatever else you want.

Vegan Black Bean Tacos

- 10 or more • CORN TORTILLA
- 1 to 2 tablespoons • COCONUT OIL
- REFRIED BLACK BEANS
- CHEDDAR CHEESE, shredded
- LETTUCE, chopped
- TOMATOES, chopped
- ONIONS, chopped
- SPROUTS for topping
- SALSA
- LIME

In a good fry pan, heat coconut oil.

Place one or two corn tortillas into pan and fry for a moment. Turn, add beans and cheese in the middle.

Fold one side of the taco over, and fry, then flip over and fry the other side. You can tell when they are done when the cheese starts to melt and tortillas start to brown. Remove from pan.

Fill with lettuce, tomatoes, onions, sprouts, your favorite salsa, and a spritz of lime.

Yum!

Chicken Tamale Casserole

1 cup (4 oz.) pre-shredded ●4-CHEESE MEXICAN BLEND, divided
⅓ cup ●MILK
2 ●EGGS
1 teaspoon ground ●CUMIN
⅛ teaspoon ground ●RED PEPPER
1 (14¾-ounce) can ●CORN, cream style
Homemade, or mix ●CORN MUFFINS
1 (4-ounce) can ●GREEN CHILES, chopped drained
●COOKING SPRAY
1 (10-ounce) can ●RED ENCHILADA SAUCE
2 cups ●CHICKEN BREAST, cooked, shredded
½ cup fat-free ●SOUR CREAM

Preheat oven to 400°.

Combine ¼ cup of the cheese and next 7 ingredients (through chilies) in a large bowl, stirring just until moist. Pour mixture into a 13 x 9–inch baking dish coated with cooking spray.

Bake at 400° for 15 minutes or until set. Pierce entire surface liberally with a fork; pour enchilada sauce over top. Top with chicken; sprinkle with remaining ¾ cup cheese. Bake at 400° for 15 minutes or until cheese melts.

Remove from oven; let stand 5 minutes. Cut into 8 pieces; top each serving with 1 tablespoon sour cream.

Taco and Quesadilla Bar

- FRESH FLOUR TORTILLAS
- JALAPENOS
- CHILI
- BLACK BEANS
- GRILLED CHICKEN
- GRILLED STEAK
- BELL PEPPERS
- ONIONS
- CHEESE
- OLIVES
- HOMEMADE SALSA

On the serving bar, line up bowls with as many different ingredients as you can.

Start building your quesadilla with two large tortillas on a plate. Load up one tortilla with choice of fillings and then place 2nd tortilla on the top. Hand over to the "chef" at the end of the bar to give it a quick frying on both top and bottom. Oh my...

Yum!

Be creative and fix up a soup bar with 4 different soups. Go to my soup recipe page and find the most delicious soups ever!

South of the Border

1 large, low-carb	• WHOLE GRAIN TORTILLA
2 slices	• MONTEREY JACK CHEESE
3 slices	• TOMATOES
	• SPROUTS
	• SALT & PEPPER

Place tortilla on a paper plate.

Lay cheese slices on top of tortilla and microwave until cheese is melted.

Remove from microwave. Add tomatoes, sprouts and salt & pepper to taste.

You can add salsa or veggies—but this is so good you won't want to.

Yum!

My notes...

My notes...

Salads & Dressings

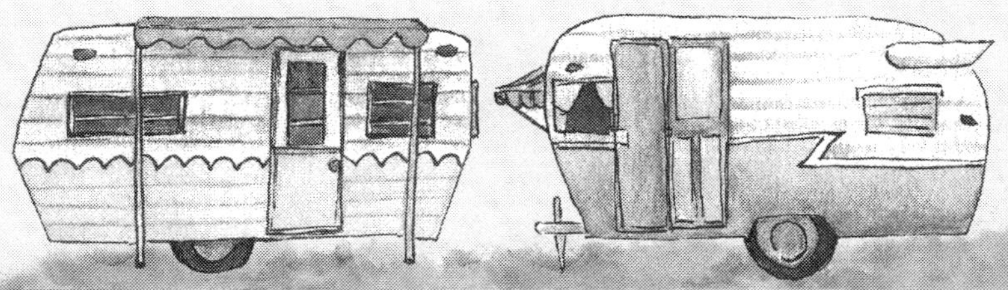

Cucumber Salad
with Tomato & Sweet Onion

Salad

4 •CUCUMBERS, any type

2 •TOMATOES, medium, sweet, vine ripened

½ •SWEET ONION, large

Dressing

3 to 4 tablespoons •WHITE BALSAMIC VINEGAR

3 tablespoons •OLIVE OIL

•GARLIC SALT & PEPPER to taste

Peel cucumbers if necessary, and slice into 1/16" rounds. Lately I have been using lemon cucumbers—*yum!*

Slice or cut tomatoes into small wedges.

Slice and cut onions.

For the dressing, whisk all ingredients together well. For best results, place dressing in the refrigerator for a few hours before serving, stirring occasionally.

Combine in a serving bowl and gently pour dressing, mixing well.

Best eatin' ever!!

Corn Salad

8 ears raw	●CORN, husked, cleaned
3 large	●TOMATOES, diced
1 large	●ONION, diced
¼ cup fresh	●BASIL, chopped
¼ cup	●OLIVE OIL or GRAPE SEED OIL
2 tablespoons	●WHITE BALSAMIC VINEGAR
	●SALT & PEPPER to taste

Bring a large pot of lightly salted water to a boil.

Cook corn in boiling water for 7 to 10 minutes, or until desired tenderness.

Drain, cool, and cut kernels off the cob with a sharp knife.

In a large bowl, toss together the corn, tomatoes, onion, basil, oil, vinegar, salt and pepper.

Chill until serving.

Pasta Salad

Salad

1 bag	● PASTA TWISTS, Barilla brand
1 bag	● VEGGIE TWISTS
1 whole	● MAUI SWEET ONION, chopped
½	● RED BELL PEPPER, chopped
½	● GREEN BELL PEPPER, chopped
½ bag	● FROZEN PEAS
2 stalks	● CELERY, chopped
12 ounce bag	● FROZEN CORN
1 whole bunch	● PARSLEY, chopped
2 cups cooked	● HAM, diced
½ cup	● BEETS, sliced

Cook pasta, following directions on bag. Cool pasta and place in large bowl. Add all ingredients to pasta and mix well with hands. Add dressing and then mix again.

Dressing

2 packages	● ITALIAN SALAD DRESSING MIX
2 tablespoons	● TERIYAKI SAUCE
1 to 2 teaspoons of each	● CELERY SALT, BASIL, and HONEY

Follow directions for dressing mix using rice or balsamic vinegar. Whisk well together, taste, and add more spices as needed.

Potato Salad

4 pounds	●RED POTATOES, washed
1 whole	●MAUI SWEET ONION, chopped
1 whole	●PARSLEY bunch, chopped
1 to 2 cups	●VEGENAISE (made with grape seed oil)
4 stalks	●CELERY, chopped
4 tablespoons	●MUSTARD
2 tablespoons	●CELERY SALT
3 tablespoons	●SALAD SUPREME SEASONING (any brand)
2 tablespoons	●DRIED BASIL
2 heaping tablespoons	●SWEET PICKLE RELISH
	●GARLIC SALT & PEPPER

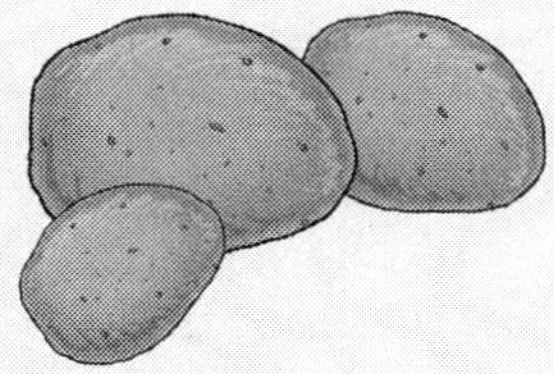

Boil potatoes until soft, but not mushy. Remove from heat and let stand for 15 minutes. You will notice that some of the skin has begun to peel away. Peel off the skin that comes off easily, and leave the rest of the skin on. Cool potatoes to room temperature.

Cut potatoes into cubes, place in a large bowl with the other ingredients, and mix well using your hands or a large spoon. Taste and add extra salt as needed.

Refrigerate for 2 hours and devour!

Shredded Tex-Mex Layered Salad

- ROMAINE LETTUCE, finely chopped
- RED ONION, sliced
- GREEN ONIONS, chopped
- BELL PEPPERS, sliced (red or green, fresh or grilled)
- BLACK BEANS
- CHEESE OF CHOICE, shredded
- CHICKEN or BEEF, shredded
- DRESSING (See Creamy Lime Dressing on page 66)

Layer all ingredients, making at least two to three layers. You may add anything you like to this salad; don't be afraid to try new ideas!

Drizzle Creamy Lime Dressing over salad and serve immediately.

Oriental Cole Slaw

Salad

4 to 8 cups	●CABBAGE, shredded. (I encourage you to use whatever type of cabbage you like—I like Napa cabbage.)
6	●GREEN ONIONS, chopped
1 tablespoon	●TOASTED SESAME SEEDS
½ cup	●TOASTED ALMONDS (optional)
1 cup	●RAMEN NOODLES, crushed
½ cup	●CELERY, chopped
	●CHICKEN PIECES, grilled or cooked, sliced or chopped

Dressing

1 tablespoon	●MAPLE SYRUP
1 teaspoon	●GARLIC SALT or to taste
½ teaspoon	●PEPPER or to taste
⅛ cup	●SEASONED RICE VINEGAR
⅛ cup	●SESAME OIL

Layer cabbage, celery, green onions and chicken. Add toasted sesame seeds, toasted almonds and ramen noodles just before adding dressing. Toss and serve immediately for best flavor and "crunch."

To toast almonds and sesame seeds, bake at 350° for 10 minutes in a single layer on a cookie sheet.

Dressing: Mix dressing ingredients in a small jar and store in refrigerator until ready to serve.

Fresh Fruit Salad

Cut up...

WATERMELON,
CANTALOUPE,
STRAWBERRIES,
KIWI,
BLUEBERRIES,
ORANGES
GRAPES
STRAWBERRIES
PINEAPPLE...

and any other fruit you like. The flavors will blend and will be delicious.

Layered Berry & Melon Salad

In a beautiful glass bowl, layer watermelon, honeydew melon, cantaloupe, raspberries, strawberries, blueberries, grapes, etc.

Squeeze a little lime juice and drizzle a little pure maple syrup on the berries. Keep layering until you get to the top.

Strawberry & Spinach Salad
with Chicken

2 bunches	●BABY SPINACH, rinsed
4 cups sliced	●STRAWBERRIES
½ cup	●OLIVE OIL
¼ cup	●BALSAMIC VINEGAR
¼ cup	●MAPLE SYRUP
¼ teaspoon	●PAPRIKA
2 tablespoons	●SESAME SEEDS
1 tablespoon	●POPPY SEEDS
2 cups	●CHICKEN, cooked and shredded

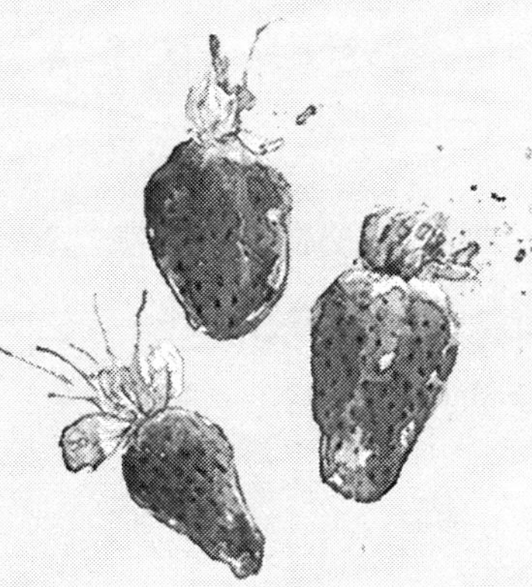

In a large bowl, toss together the spinach and strawberries.

In a medium bowl, whisk together the oil, vinegar, syrup, paprika, sesame seeds, and poppy seeds.

Pour over the spinach and strawberries, and toss to coat.

You can also add chicken or shrimp.

White Balsamic Salad Dressing

- WHITE BALSAMIC VINEGAR
- OLIVE OIL
- GARLIC SALT and PEPPER to taste.

Combine equal parts of white balsamic vinegar and olive oil; mix well. This is my very favorite salad dressing!!

Creamy Lime Dressing

2 tablespoons fresh	●CILANTRO, chopped
1 tablespoon	●RED WINE VINEGAR
1 teaspoon	●LIME ZEST
¼ cup	●LIME JUICE
½ cup	●SOUR CREAM (can use non-fat)
1 clove	●GARLIC, smashed
1 tablespoon	●HONEY
½ cup	●EXTRA VIRGIN OLIVE OIL or FLAX OIL
	●SALT & PEPPER to taste

Blend ingredients until smooth and refrigerate. Drizzle dressing over salad and serve immediately.

Delicious
Lemon Salad Dressing

2 •LEMONS (or more)

1/8 cup •OLIVE OIL or GRAPE SEED OIL

•GARLIC SALT & PEPPER to taste

•PARMESAN CHEESE, optional —but this really makes the dressing!

The only way to make this dressing perfect is to actually have your salad ready to toss.

On a completely ready salad, squeeze lemons and add rest of ingredients.

Taste your salad after you toss it and see if it needs more of any of the above ingredients. It always depends on the amount of salad you use—this recipe is for at least 6 cups of salad.

Flax Oil & Balsamic Salad Dressing

½ cup •FLAX OIL

Less than ½ cup of •BALSAMIC VINEGAR

•GARLIC SALT to taste

•PARMESAN CHEESE (optional)

Mix all ingredients well. Pour over salad, and toss.

My notes...

Poultry

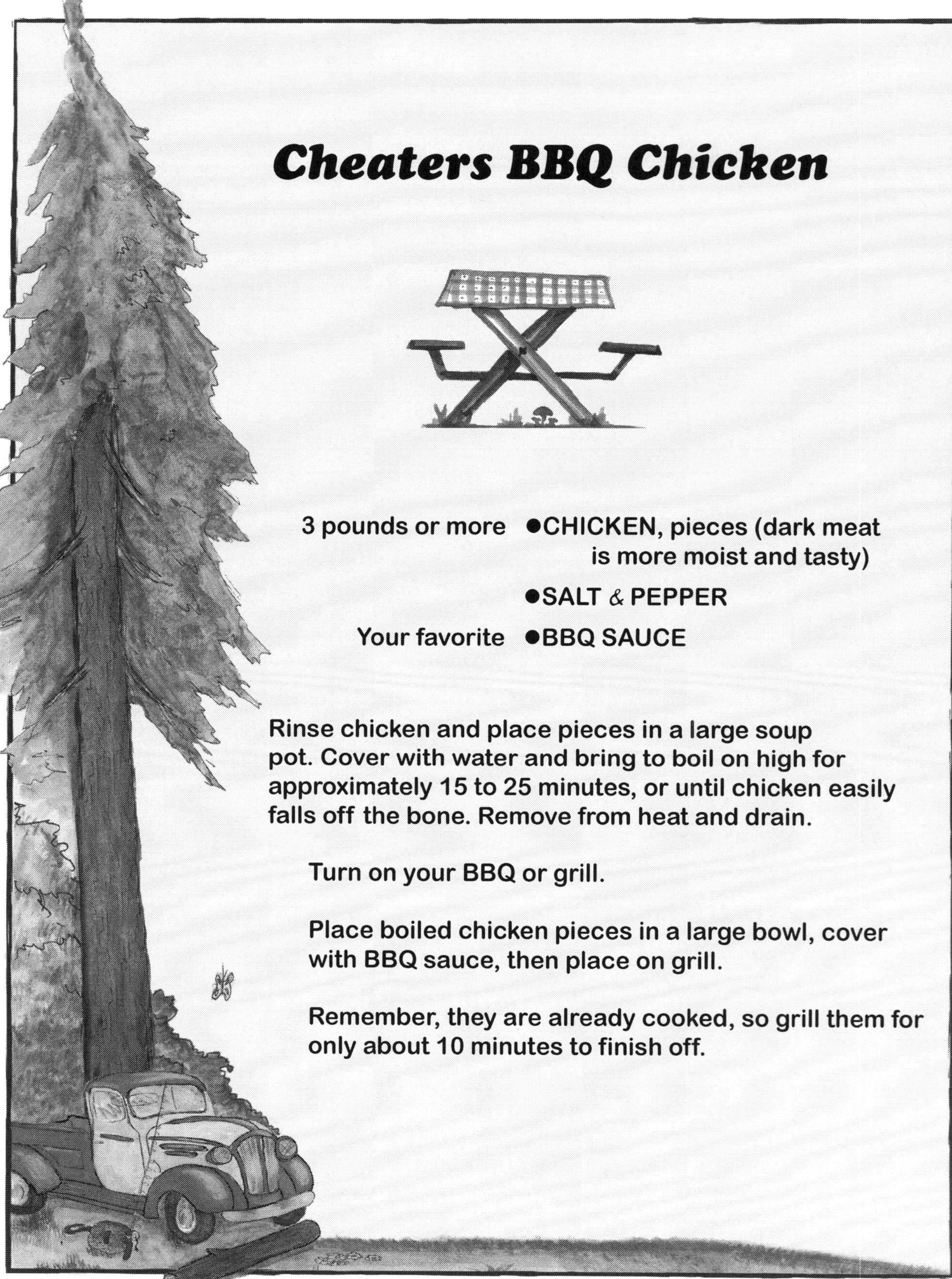

Cheaters BBQ Chicken

3 pounds or more	●CHICKEN, pieces (dark meat is more moist and tasty)
	●SALT & PEPPER
Your favorite	●BBQ SAUCE

Rinse chicken and place pieces in a large soup pot. Cover with water and bring to boil on high for approximately 15 to 25 minutes, or until chicken easily falls off the bone. Remove from heat and drain.

Turn on your BBQ or grill.

Place boiled chicken pieces in a large bowl, cover with BBQ sauce, then place on grill.

Remember, they are already cooked, so grill them for only about 10 minutes to finish off.

Teriyaki Chicken Fingers

6 pieces boneless, skinless ●CHICKEN
2 cups ●TERIYAKI SAUCE
1 cup ●WHOLE WHEAT FLOUR
¼ cup ●COCONUT OIL

Rinse chicken and pat dry then cut into 1 to 2 inch thick strips.

In a large plastic bag, pour 2 cups of your favorite teriyaki sauce and add chicken. Leave in refrigerator to marinate overnight.

The next day, roll chicken in flour until it is covered.

In a frying pan over medium-high heat, heat the coconut oil and place floured chicken in it and fry until golden brown. Place on a paper towel to let drain. Eat hot or cold!

Curry Chicken

2 tablespoons	● OAT FLOUR
6 boneless, skinless (approx. 6 oz. each)	● CHICKEN BREASTS
3 tablespoons	● COCONUT OIL
4 tablespoons	● BUTTER
1	● SWEET ONION, finely chopped
2	● GARLIC CLOVES, minced
2 to 3 teaspoons	● CURRY POWDER (medium to hot)
2 tablespoons	● FRONTIER CHICKEN BROTH POWDER or BOUILLON
	● GARLIC SALT & PEPPER to taste
6 cups, cooked	● BROWN RICE (cooked in Chicken Broth)

Rinse chicken and pat dry. Flour chicken.

In a large skillet or BBQ grill over medium heat, fry chicken in half of the oil and butter until cooked. After slightly cooled, chop chicken and set aside.

In a skillet, melt butter over medium heat and then add oil. Sauté garlic and onion, then add rice, chicken and curry powder.

As if you were cooking in a wok, stir rice and chicken with two wooden spoons.

You can use the Frontier Chicken Broth Powder instead of salt, and if you need to, add more garlic salt and pepper to taste.

Salsa Lime Chicken

1 whole	●CHICKEN, or 8 to 10 pieces
	●GARLIC SALT to taste
1 clove	●GARLIC
¼ cup	●LIME JUICE (bottled or fresh)
2 cups	●SALSA, fresh homemade, or favorite store-bought

Preheat oven to 500°.

Rinse chicken. Place in baking pan (that you can cover) and sprinkle with garlic salt.

Cover with chopped garlic, lime juice and salsa.

Bake uncovered for 30 minutes or until lightly browned.

Cover and bake for an additional 45 minutes.

Serve over barley, couscous, brown rice or vegetables and garnish with fresh salsa.

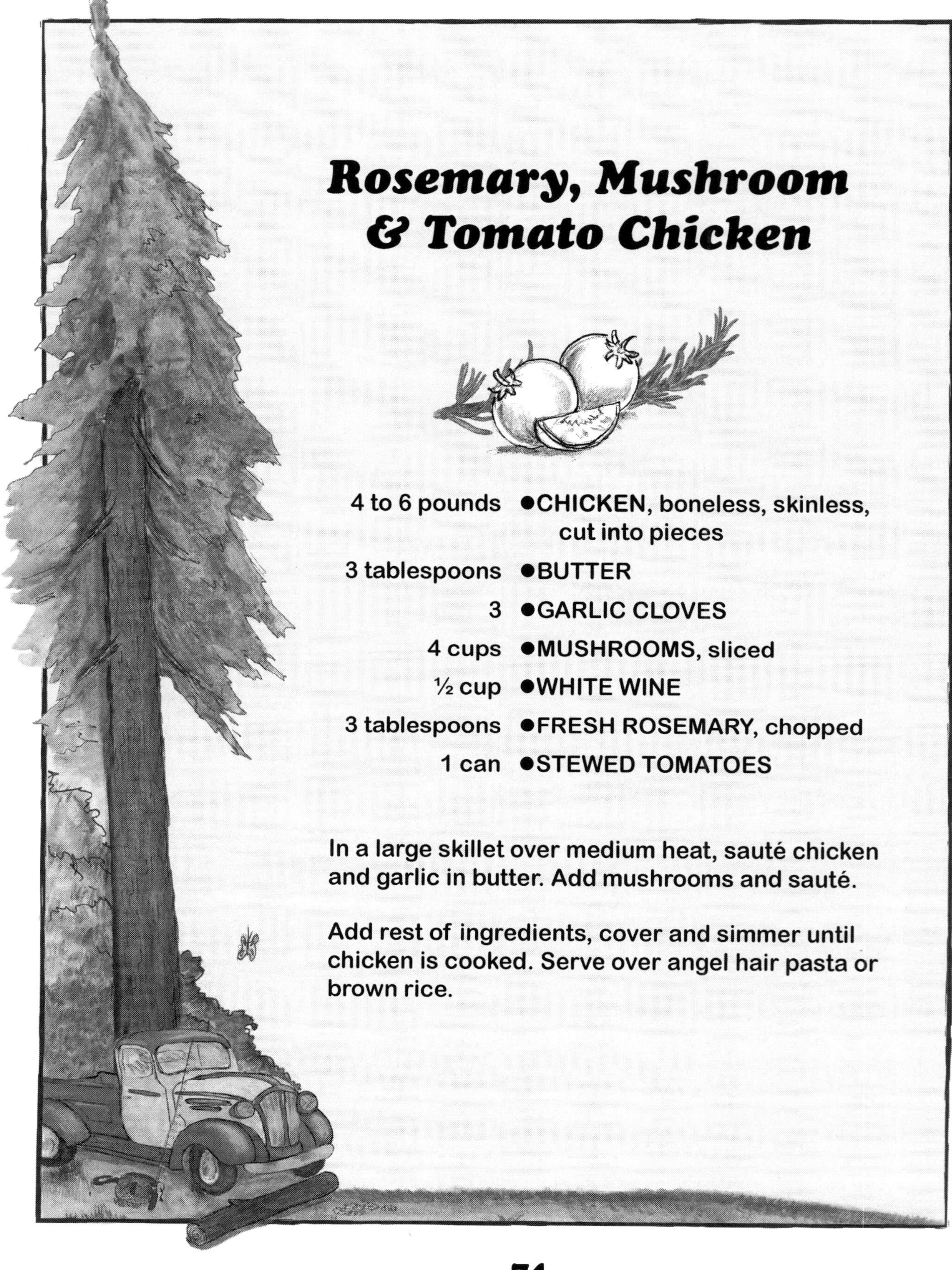

Rosemary, Mushroom & Tomato Chicken

4 to 6 pounds	•CHICKEN, boneless, skinless, cut into pieces
3 tablespoons	•BUTTER
3	•GARLIC CLOVES
4 cups	•MUSHROOMS, sliced
½ cup	•WHITE WINE
3 tablespoons	•FRESH ROSEMARY, chopped
1 can	•STEWED TOMATOES

In a large skillet over medium heat, sauté chicken and garlic in butter. Add mushrooms and sauté.

Add rest of ingredients, cover and simmer until chicken is cooked. Serve over angel hair pasta or brown rice.

Chicken Scaloppini with Mushrooms

6	●CHICKEN BREAST HALVES or dark meat, boned and skinned
5 tablespoons	●UNSALTED BUTTER
5 tablespoons	●COCONUT OIL
½ pound	●FRESH MUSHROOMS, sliced
2 tablespoons	●GREEN ONIONS, chopped
¼ cup	●DRY WHITE WINE
⅓ cup organic	●CHICKEN BROTH
½ cup	●HEAVY CREAM
	●GARLIC SALT & PEPPER to taste

Place chicken pieces between 2 sheets of waxed paper and pound with a mallet. Try to pound to a uniform thickness.

Heat 2 tablespoons each of the butter and oil in a sauté pan. Add the mushrooms and sauté until tender, about 4 to 5 minutes. Remove mushrooms with slotted spoon and set aside.

Heat the remaining 3 tablespoons each of butter and oil over medium heat. Add the chicken and sauté, turning once, until browned, about 4 to 5 minutes total cooking time. Remove chicken and reserve.

Add the shallots or green onion to the pan and cook, scraping the pan bottom with a wooden spoon to loosen browned bits. Until tender, about 4 minutes. Add the white wine and chicken stock, bring to a boil, reduce heat to a simmer, and cook until the liquids are reduced by half. Stir in the cream and garlic salt and pepper to taste. Add mushrooms and chicken, simmer to reheat. Serve immediately.

Sautéed Chicken
with Coconut Cream Gravy

8 pieces	●CHICKEN (I prefer dark meat, but use whatever you want)
6 cloves	●GARLIC, minced
3 tablespoons	●COCONUT OIL
1 can	●COCONUT MILK, Thai brand
2 cups	●FRESH TOMATOES, diced
	●GARLIC SALT & PEPPER to taste

In a large saucepan heat coconut oil until very hot. Add minced garlic and chicken pieces. Cook chicken well on each side. When done, remove from pan and leave juices to sauté tomatoes until they break down.

Add coconut milk, garlic salt and pepper to taste. Simmer for approximately 5 minutes, stirring the whole time. If you want the gravy thicker, simmer longer.

Place chicken back into the gravy, heat and serve over a bed of Quinoa.

Yum!

Stir-fry Chicken
with Brown Rice & Veggies

2 tablespoons	●COCONUT OIL, divided
½	●SWEET ONION, chopped
2-4	●GARLIC CLOVES, finely minced
2 pounds	●CHICKEN, dark meat—or white meat if you prefer, chopped in small pieces
1 head	●BROCCOLI, stems removed, finely diced
1 dozen	●MUSHROOMS, sliced
3	●CARROTS, peeled and julienned
1/4 pound	●GREEN BEANS, diced
1 head	●BOK CHOY, chopped
2 to 3 tablespoons	●TERIYAKI SAUCE with GINGER
	●DARK SESAME OIL, to taste, optional

Heat 1 tablespoon coconut oil in a sauté pan over medium heat. When oil is hot, add onion, garlic and stir.

Add chopped chicken and lightly brown to cook. Remove from pan, set aside.

Heat remaining tablespoon of oil in a wok over high heat. Add the vegetables and teriyaki sauce. Stir-fry quickly until the vegetables begin to soften.

Add the chicken, combine well and continue to cook for 2 to 3 minutes. Add sesame oil, if desired and stir to mix. Serve immediately over brown rice.

Yum!

Chicken Stewoup

8 to 10 pieces	●CHICKEN, washed
1 whole	●SWEET ONION, diced
1 bunch	●FRESH PARSLEY, minced
5 tablespoons	●DRIED BASIL
2 cups	●CARROTS, diced
2 boxes	●CHICKEN BROTH, organic
3 tablespoons	●COCONUT OIL
4 cups or more	●BROWN RICE
	●GARLIC SALT & PEPPER to taste

In a large fry pan, brown chicken in coconut oil.

Place browned chicken into large soup pot. Add all of the ingredients except chicken broth. Once everything is in the soup pot, add chicken broth to cover all ingredients plus 2 inches more.

Simmer for 45 minutes, or until chicken starts to fall off the bones. Garlic salt and pepper to taste.

In a separate pot, make brown rice. (I like brown minute rice as it cooks up perfectly every time and only takes minutes to make).

Add rice to the stew, or the stew to the rice—all depending on how thick or thin you want the stewoup!

Yum!

Chicken on a Stick

3 to 4 four pounds ●BONELESS CHICKEN
1 bottle ●YOSHIDA'S TERIYAKI SAUCE

Rinse and pat dry chicken.

Cut into strips and place in large Zip-lock bag with teriyaki sauce. Close bag and place in refrigerator overnight.

The next day, pour off teriyaki sauce and discard. Thread marinated chicken strips onto skewers.

Heat grill on high for 10 minutes then turn to medium.

Place chicken skewers onto grill and roll over every 5 minutes until done.

Yum!

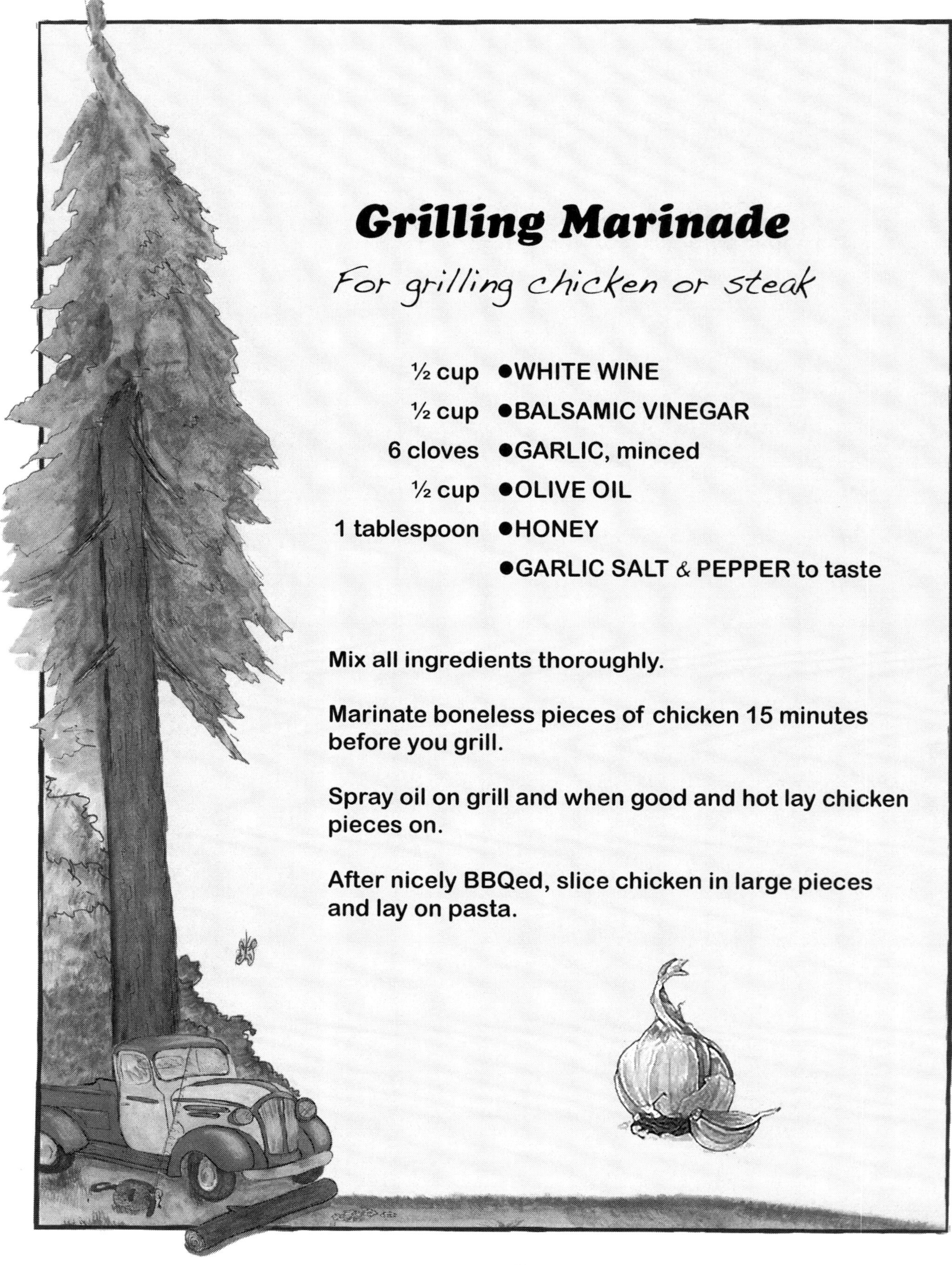

Grilling Marinade

For grilling chicken or steak

½ cup	●WHITE WINE
½ cup	●BALSAMIC VINEGAR
6 cloves	●GARLIC, minced
½ cup	●OLIVE OIL
1 tablespoon	●HONEY
	●GARLIC SALT & PEPPER to taste

Mix all ingredients thoroughly.

Marinate boneless pieces of chicken 15 minutes before you grill.

Spray oil on grill and when good and hot lay chicken pieces on.

After nicely BBQed, slice chicken in large pieces and lay on pasta.

My notes...

My notes...

Seafood

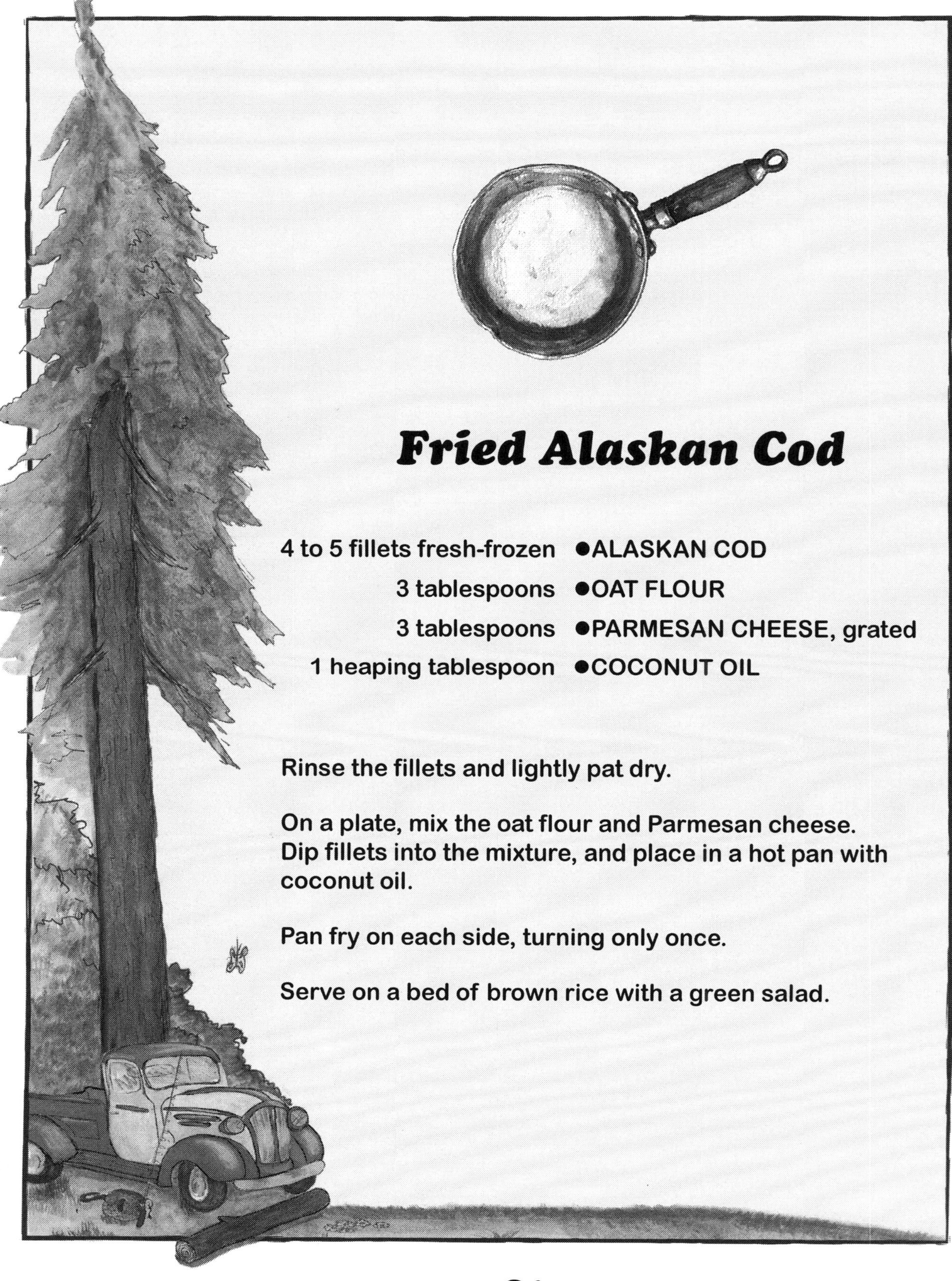

Fried Alaskan Cod

4 to 5 fillets fresh-frozen •ALASKAN COD
3 tablespoons •OAT FLOUR
3 tablespoons •PARMESAN CHEESE, grated
1 heaping tablespoon •COCONUT OIL

Rinse the fillets and lightly pat dry.

On a plate, mix the oat flour and Parmesan cheese. Dip fillets into the mixture, and place in a hot pan with coconut oil.

Pan fry on each side, turning only once.

Serve on a bed of brown rice with a green salad.

Parmesan Crusted
Alaskan Cod

2 pounds	●ALASKAN COD (or other fish)
½ cup	●PARMESAN CHEESE, grated
½ cup	●OAT BRAN
2	●EGGS
2 tablespoons	●VIRGIN COCONUT OIL

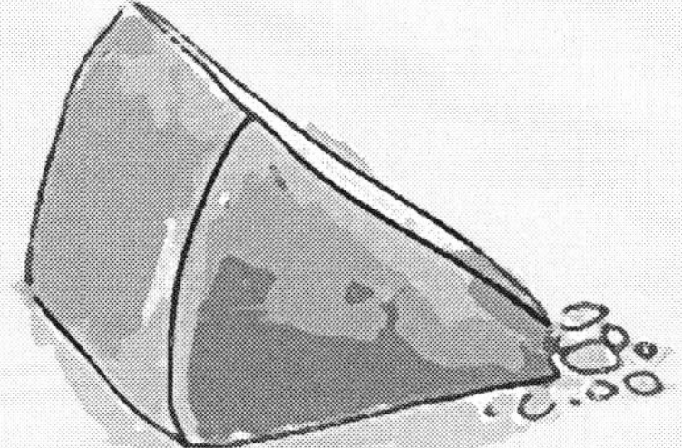

On a plate, mix Parmesan cheese and oat bran.

In a large wide bowl, beat 2 eggs.

Heat a saucepan and add 3 heaping tablespoons of coconut oil.

Wash and pat dry cod.

Dip cod into egg and then into Parmesan bran mix.

Gently place cod into heated coconut oil. On medium heat, let the cod brown on one side, then gently turn over. It is better to use cod pieces that are of uniform thickness and not too thick.

This crust is so delicious that you don't need salt or seasoning.

Yum!

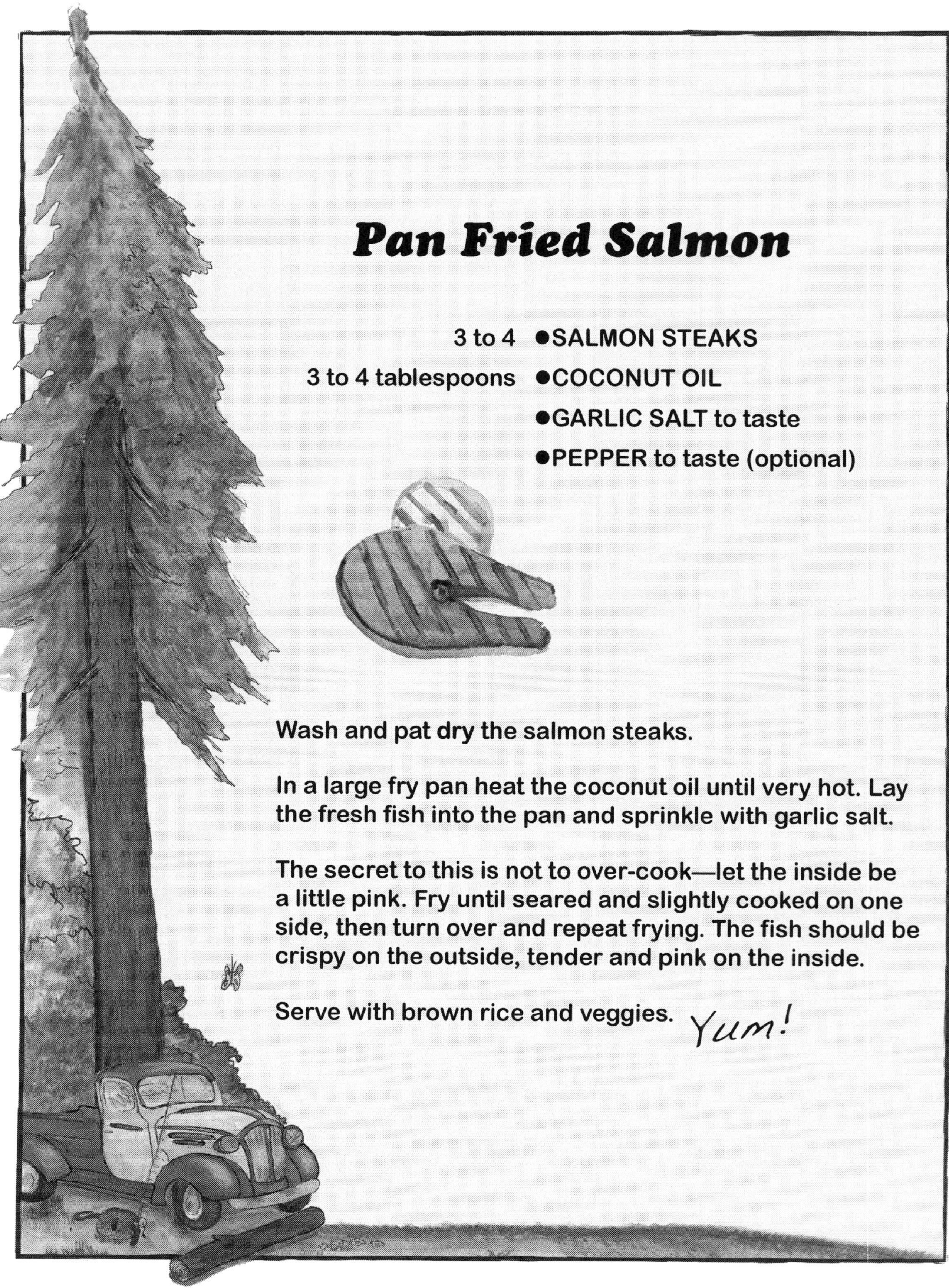

Pan Fried Salmon

3 to 4	●SALMON STEAKS
3 to 4 tablespoons	●COCONUT OIL
	●GARLIC SALT to taste
	●PEPPER to taste (optional)

Wash and pat dry the salmon steaks.

In a large fry pan heat the coconut oil until very hot. Lay the fresh fish into the pan and sprinkle with garlic salt.

The secret to this is not to over-cook—let the inside be a little pink. Fry until seared and slightly cooked on one side, then turn over and repeat frying. The fish should be crispy on the outside, tender and pink on the inside.

Serve with brown rice and veggies. *Yum!*

Teriyaki Grilled Salmon

Fillet pieces
- SALMON
- COCONUT OIL Spray
- GARLIC SALT, to taste
- TERIYAKI SAUCE

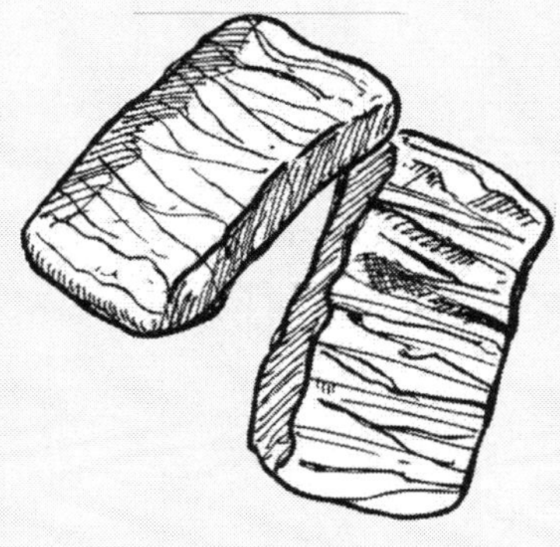

Saturate BBQ grill with coconut oil spray. Turn on heat.

Spray olive oil on skin side of fillet and place on a hot grill, sprinkle with garlic salt.

You will cook the fillet mostly on the skin side—then turn fillet over, remove skin, and sprinkle with garlic salt.

When you are ready to finish (otherwise it will burn), brush teriyaki sauce on and turn fillet again. Brush on the other side, turn again. Whamo!—done in a few minutes—don't overcook.

Salmon Cakes

4 pounds (approx.)	●SALMON, deboned, baked or poached
½ cup good quality	●MAYONNAISE or VEGENAISE
⅛ cup	●TERIYAKI SAUCE with GINGER
2 tablespoons	●DILL WEED
2	●EGGS
2 teaspoons	●GARLIC SALT (more or less)
½ cup	●OAT BRAN
⅛ cup	●OAT FLOUR
¼ cup	●COCONUT OIL

Pull the bones from the salmon and shred into a bowl.

Add the mayonnaise, teriyaki sauce with ginger, dill weed and eggs. Mix well. Add garlic salt to taste.

Form patties, the size of a good size hamburger, patting the sides. Combine the oat bran, oat flour and garlic salt (to taste) in a bowl and dip the patties into the mixture.

Place coconut oil into a large skillet over medium heat. Add patties and brown one side. Turn only once and brown second side.

These delicious Salmon Cakes are even great cold.

Herb Crusted Calamari

4 ●CALAMARI STEAKS

3 ●EGGS

●COCONUT OIL

Dried ●DILL WEED

●GARLIC SALT & PEPPER to taste

In a bowl, beat eggs.

Heat a large fry pan with 1 to 2 tablespoons of coconut oil. Let the coconut oil get hot.

Wash calamari steaks and pat dry. Dip steaks into egg and place directly into hot pan of oil. Sprinkle with dill and garlic salt. Lightly brown one side, then turn. Turn only once.

Place on a bed of rice. *Yum!*

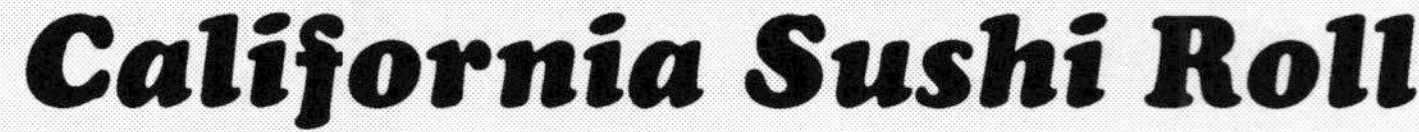

California Sushi Roll

1 cup ●SUSHI RICE, Calrose short grain
¼ cup ●SEASONED GOURMET RICE VINEGAR
1 ●AVOCADO
1 ●ENGLISH CUCUMBER
½ cup ●CRAB MEAT (real or imitation)
●MAYONNAISE to taste
●SUSHI PAPER (nori seaweed)
●SOY SAUCE, low sodium
●WASABI
●PICKLED GINGER

Rinse rice under running water until water is almost clear, and then cook with 1 cup of water in a rice cooker. If you don't own a rice cooker, simmer rice in a pot, covered, for 15 to 20 minutes or until done.

You can use brown rice but it does not have the "stickiness" that is convenient for rolling the sushi—try a combination.

Place cooked rice in a bowl. Add the vinegar and mix gently while fanning the rice to cool it. Set aside.

Peel the cucumber, then slice into long, thin strips. Also peel and slice the avocado into strips. Set aside.

Continued...

Mix crab with mayonnaise. Set aside.

Place a seaweed sheet (nori) shiny-side down on a bamboo mat. Spoon some rice on the nori sheet and spread to the edges, but leave about 1 inch at the furthest end from you.

On the end closest to you, put a line of crab mixture, cucumber and avocado across the rice.

Roll the mat beginning with the edge closest to you. Continue to roll until you reach the reserved inch you left at the furthest edge. Put some water across the reserved portion of the nori, and roll it completely over. The water will keep the nori edges together. Press down firmly on the edge to ensure a tight adhesion. Release the bamboo mat and pull it back towards you, leaving the sushi roll in place.

Dip a long, sharp knife in cold water to prevent it from sticking to the sushi rice. Slice the roll into small pieces. Make the second roll using the same method.

Serve immediately with soy sauce, wasabi and pickled ginger.

Meals on a Grill

Cook anything this way!

- FISH FILLETS of your choice (salmon is best), CHICKEN OR BEEF
- Large pieces HEAVY DUTY ALUMINUM FOIL
- GARLIC SALT
- BUTTER
- TERIYAKI SAUCE (optional)
- POTATOES, thinly sliced
- VEGGIES, thinly sliced

Place butter, meat, potatoes and veggies in the middle of the foil. Sprinkle with garlic salt, herbs or even teriyaki sauce.

Form a packet rolling the sides tightly to prevent juices from leaking out.

Place the foil packet directly on the fire or very hot grill and cook for 10 minutes.

For grilled veggies or potatoes, repeat the same process.

My notes...

My notes...

Meat

Dianne's Quick Stew

3 to 4 pounds	●STEW MEAT, cut into ½-inch cubes
2 tablespoons	●BUTTER
2 tablespoons	●COCONUT OIL
4	●CARROTS, chopped
8	●RED POTATOES, cubed
8 to 14 ounces fresh	●SALSA

In a large skillet, melt butter and coconut oil. Heat pan until hot then add the meat and brown it. Sprinkle with garlic salt and pepper to taste, turn heat on low and pour fresh salsa over the meat.

Add potatoes and carrots, cover and simmer for approximately 30 to 40 minutes or until the meat is tender.

This is excellent over brown rice or mashed potatoes. I love grilled asparagus as a side dish!

Cowboy Stew

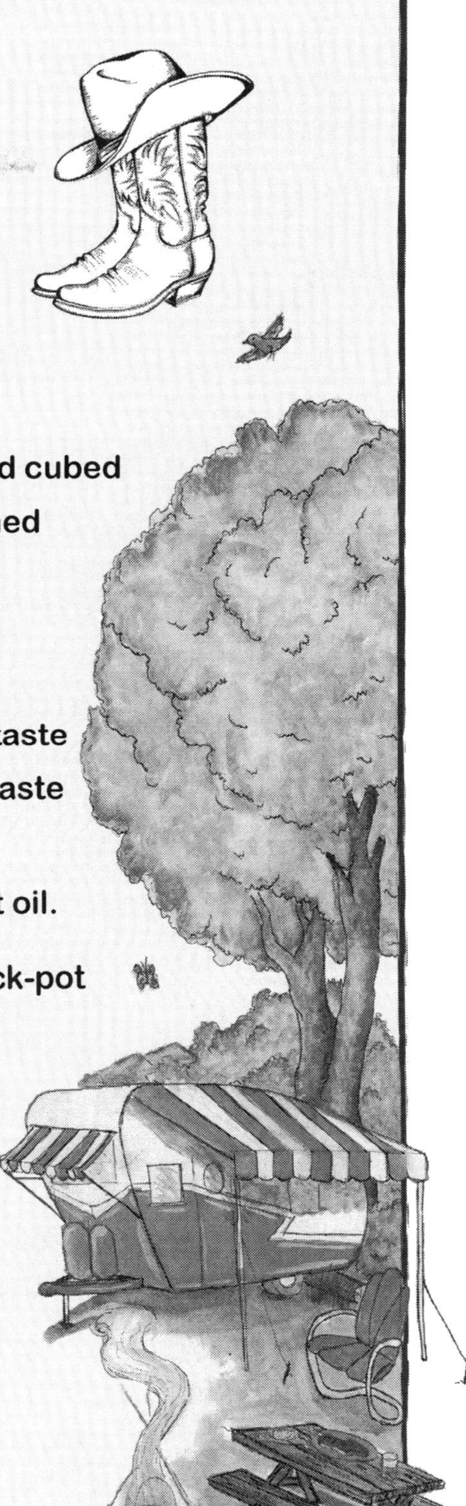

	●BUTTER or COCONUT OIL
4 to 5 lbs.	●STEW MEAT, cubed
2 lbs.	●RED POTATOES, washed and cubed
1 bag of small	●CARROTS, peeled and washed
½	●SWEET ONION, chopped
2 cloves	●GARLIC, minced
16 oz.	●SALSA, medium heat
	●GARLIC SALT & PEPPER to taste
2 to 3 tablespoons	●PURE MAPLE SYRUP, or to taste

Brown the stew meat in some butter or coconut oil.

Place browned meat with all the juices in a crock-pot or stew pot and add the remaining ingredients.

Set crock-pot on high heat for 6 to 7 hours. If using a stew pot, place in oven at 325° for approximately 3 to 4 hours. The stew is done when the meat falls apart.

Serve with a big green salad and homemade corn bread.

Yum!

Delicious Braised Beef

	●COCONUT OIL, for sautéing and drizzling
4	●SWEET ONIONS, very thinly sliced
6 cloves	●GARLIC, very thinly sliced
4 pounds	●CHUCK, BOTTOM ROUND or TOP SIRLOIN STEAK
	●GARLIC SALT
Freshly ground	●BLACK PEPPER
1 cup	●OAT BRAN or OAT FLOUR
1 32-ounce can	●ITALIAN TOMATOES, sliced or roughly crushed
2 tablespoons	●THYME, fresh, chopped
A few fresh	●BASIL LEAVES, torn

Preheat the oven to 325°.

Heat a large skillet over medium heat and add a thin layer of coconut oil.

Dredge meat in flour and place in hot oil. Sprinkle well with garlic salt. Brown all sides, then place in Dutch oven.

In the skillet, with remaining hot oil, add onions and sauté until translucent. Add remaining ingredients and briefly sauté, and then pour all sautéed ingredients on top of the meat. Cover Dutch oven and roast until the meat is very tender—about 4 hours.

This is a great meal to make ahead of time. You can also prepare this dish in a crock pot! Serve on homemade mashed potatoes.

Braised Short Ribs

¼ cup	●WHOLE WHEAT FLOUR
	●SALT & PEPPER to taste
8 pieces bone-in beef	●SHORT RIBS
⅛ cup	●COCONUT OIL
1 cup	●RED WINE
	●FRESH THYME

In a large skillet, heat oil over medium heat.

Dip short ribs in flour and salt and pepper. Place ribs in hot oil and fry, turn only once. Brown both sides, add remaining ingredients, then cover and simmer over low heat for 20 minutes. (You can also cook in a crock pot.)

Serve with rice or mashed potatoes and veggies.

Cheaters

Pot Roast

This is such a simple recipe!

1 jar	●SALSA, your favorite
6	●GARLIC CLOVES, minced
4 to 6 pounds	●BEEF, high quality
	●GARLIC SALT & PEPPER to taste
	●RED POTATOES, cut into large chunks
	●CARROTS, chopped into large pieces

Sear the meat in a frying pan over medium-high heat then place in a crock pot with the potatoes, carrots, garlic and salsa. If you are camping, use a large soup pot.

Turn crock pot on high for 1 hour and then on low for 6 to 7 hours.

Serve right from the pot or you may want to mash the potatoes you just made. Either way, this meal is absolutely delicious!

Balsamic Skirt Steak

2 - 8 oz.	●SKIRT STEAKS
¼ cup	●BALSAMIC VINEGAR
4 cloves	●GARLIC, minced
	●GARLIC SALT & PEPPER to taste

Smother a quality skirt steak with balsamic vinegar, garlic, garlic salt and pepper.

Marinate steak for ten minutes, and then place on a hot grill. Turn only once.

Cheaters
BBQ Country-Style Pork Ribs

5 or more pounds	•COUNTRY PORK RIBS
	•SALT & PEPPER
Your favorite	•BBQ SAUCE

Place washed pork ribs in large soup pot. Cover ribs with water and bring to boil on high. Boil ribs for approximately 15 to 25 minutes or until they start feeling like they could easily fall apart.

Turn on your BBQ or Grill.

Pace boiled rib in a large bowl, cover with BBQ sauce, then place on grill. Remember, they are already cooked, so now grill them for only about 10 minutes to finish them off.

Maple Balsamic Pork Chops

4 tablespoons	●COCONUT OIL
6 to 8 nice, lean	●PORK CHOPS or PORK STEAKS
	●OAT FLOUR
	●GARLIC SALT & PEPPER to taste
4 tablespoons	●MAPLE SYRUP
3 tablespoons	●BALSAMIC VINEGAR

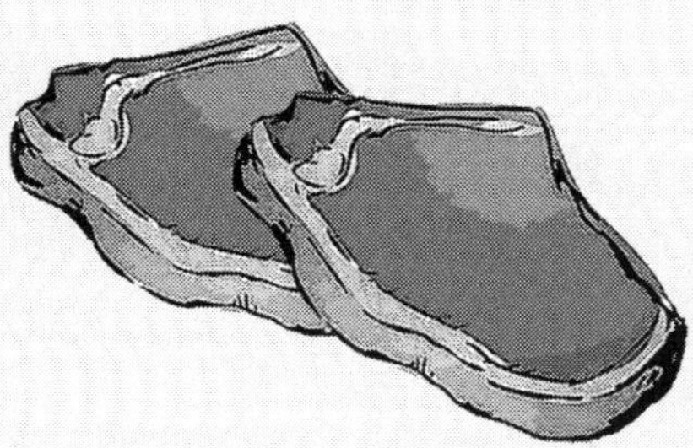

In a frying pan, heat oil over medium heat.

Dredge pork chops in flour and season with garlic salt and pepper on both sides.

Carefully lay pork chops in hot oil and brown both sides. Don't overcook.

Remove from heat onto serving platter. Drizzle with maple syrup and balsamic vinegar.

Optional: Serve with garlic mashed potatoes and vegetables. Also try a little fresh apple sauce on the side.

Cheaters Chili

1 16-oz. can	●MAPLE BAKED BEANS
2 14-oz. cans	●BLACK BEANS
1 14-oz. can	●PINTO BEANS
1 14-oz. can	●RED BEANS, small
3 lbs. lean	●GROUND BEEF
1 16-oz. can	●CRUSHED TOMATOES
3 tablespoons	●MAPLE SYRUP
1 teaspoon	●CAYENNE PEPPER
1 teaspoon	●CHILI POWDER
	●GARLIC SALT & PEPPER to taste

If you are camping, use CHILI PACKETS for flavoring.

Place ground beef in a large skillet and fry until done.

Combine the meat with rest of ingredients in a large soup pot, and warm until steaming hot.

Yum!

Fried Wontons

3 pounds low fat	●GROUND BEEF or TURKEY
2 tablespoons	●GARLIC, minced
½	●SWEET ONION, shredded
¼ cup low sodium	●SOY SAUCE plus more for dipping
4 tablespoons good quality	●TERIYAKI SAUCE
Large size	●WONTON WRAPPERS
	●COCONUT OIL

Mix meat and other ingredients well with hands.

Follow directions on wonton wrapper package for stuffing and folding.

Deep fry in coconut oil over medium-high heat until lightly browned and wontons are floating.

Drain and dip in low-sodium soy sauce.

My notes...

Side Dishes

BBQ Corn on the Cob

- CORN
- OLIVE OIL
- SALT & PEPPER
- GARLIC

Soak the Corn, husk and all, for about 15 minutes. Then gently pull back husk and remove silky strands.

Brush a little olive onto the kernels then season with the salt, pepper and garlic. Pull husk back over cob and place on grill.

Continually turn cobs to evenly char husk on all sides.

After charred, place on warming rack or sides of grill and continue to grill with lid closed for 15 minutes. Corn is done when kernels burst when pressed.

Pull back husk and enjoy!

Cauliflower Au Gratin

1 head	●CAULIFLOWER, cut into florets
2 cups	●HEAVY CREAM
½ pound	●MONTEREY JACK CHEESE, coarsely grated
2 cups	●PARMESAN, grated
	●SALT
Freshly ground	●PEPPER

Preheat oven to 400° F.

Layer the cauliflower, heavy cream, and the cheeses in a medium casserole dish and season with salt and pepper.

Roast in a saucepan or iron skillet with lid for 20 to 30 minutes or until the cauliflower is soft and the sauce has thickened slightly.

Remove from the oven and let rest for 10 minutes before serving.

Recipe can be doubled and made in a roasting pan

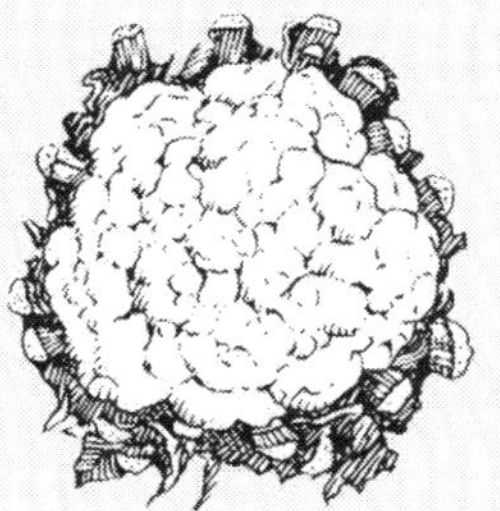

This is one of my mom's Southern dishes...

Sautéed Zucchini, Yellow Squash & Onions

- 2 to 3 ZUCCHINIS
- 2 YELLOW SQUASH
- ½ SWEET ONION
- ½ cup OAT FLOUR
- 2 tablespoons BUTTER
- 3 tablespoons COCONUT OIL
- GARLIC SALT & PEPPER

Slice the zucchinis, yellow squash and sweet onion.

Place in a bowl with the oat flour and toss.

Heat the butter and coconut oil in a skillet over medium heat. Add squash mixture and sauté until lightly browned. Add garlic salt and pepper to taste.

Sautéed Green Beans, Mushrooms & Garlic

1 lb. ●GREEN BEANS
8 ounces ●MUSHROOMS, sliced
1 tablespoon ●GARLIC, minced
4 tablespoons ●COCONUT OIL
●GARLIC SALT & PEPPER to taste

Wash and cut off ends of green beans.

Steam until crisp-tender, then submerge them in the ice water for 2 to 3 minutes.

In a large nonstick skillet, heat the oil over medium-high heat. Add the mushrooms and garlic and cook, stirring occasionally, until the mushrooms are nicely browned, about 10 to 11 minutes. Add the green beans and sauté for a couple of minutes, then add garlic salt and pepper to taste.

This is the quickest and simplest way to cook most veggies—without over cooking them.

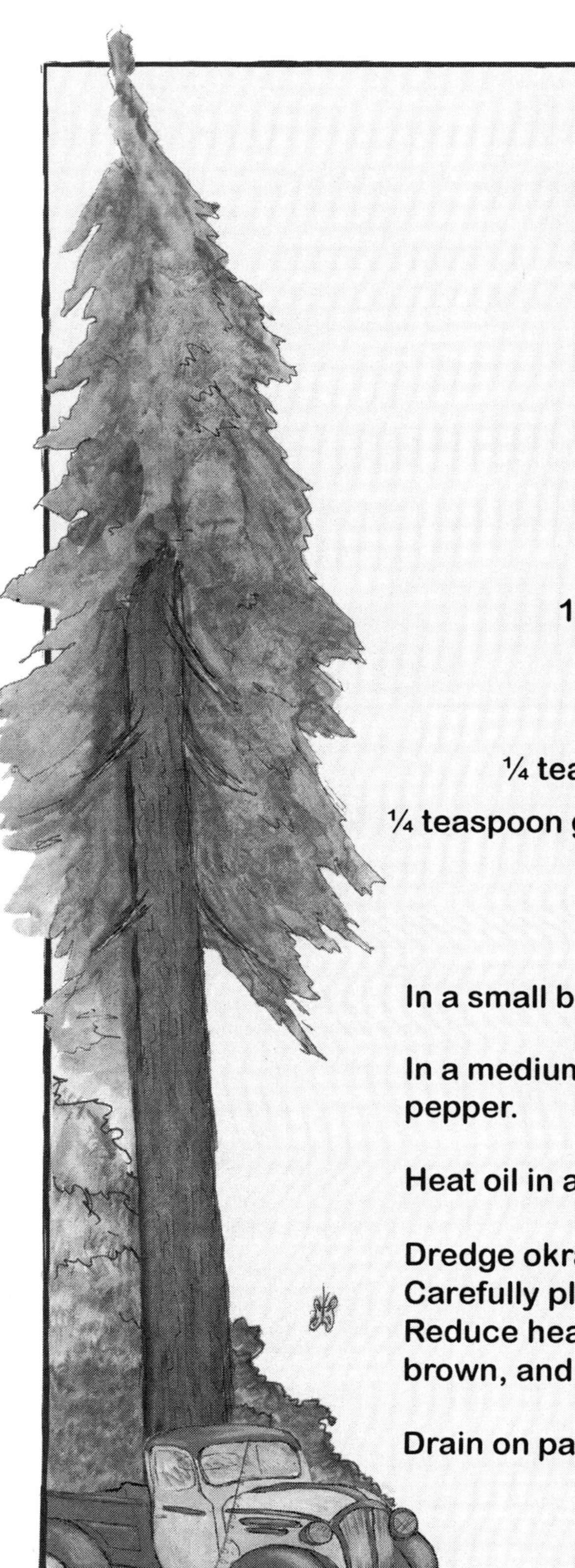

Fried Okra

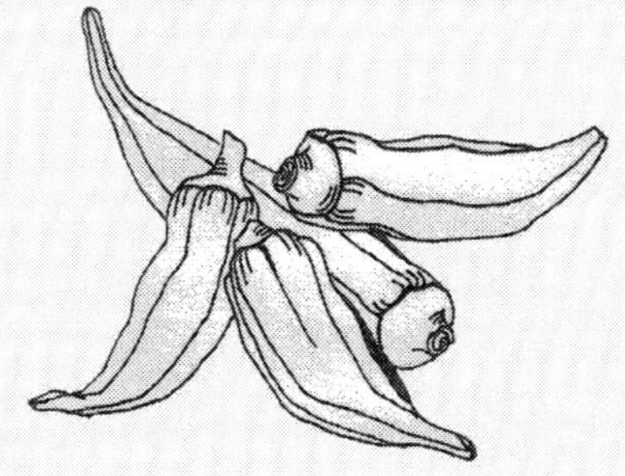

10 pods	●OKRA, sliced in ¼ inch pieces
1	●EGG, BEATEN
1 cup	●CORNMEAL
¼ teaspoon	●SALT
¼ teaspoon ground	●BLACK PEPPER
½ cup	●COCONUT OIL

In a small bowl, soak okra in egg for 5 to 10 minutes.

In a medium bowl, combine cornmeal, salt, and pepper.

Heat oil in a large skillet over medium-high heat.

Dredge okra in the cornmeal mixture, coating evenly. Carefully place okra in hot oil; stir continuously. Reduce heat to medium when okra first starts to brown, and cook until golden.

Drain on paper towels.

Grilled Veggies

2 ●Bell PEPPERS (a variety of red, orange, or green)

8 large ●MUSHROOMS

1 whole ●MAUI SWEET ONION

1 ●ZUCCHINI

⅛ cup ●BALSAMIC VINEGAR

⅛ cup ●OLIVE OIL

●GARLIC SALT & PEPPER

Slice all vegetables in ¼ inch slices.

In a bowl, combine balsamic vinegar, olive oil, salt and pepper.

Place all veggies into bowl and coat with marinade.

Get your grill very hot, and, with a pair of tongs, place veggies onto hot grill. Sometimes it is a good idea to rub some olive oil onto grill to keep veggies from sticking. Or, use a veggie basket!

Turn only once and don't over cook. These veggies are great if they are still slightly crunchy.

Stir-fry (Base)

6 cups • BROWN RICE, cooked (you can use quick rice)

1 whole • SWEET ONION, chopped

3 cups • CHINESE CABBAGE, finely chopped

3 • GARLIC CLOVES, minced

4 tablespoons • GRAPE SEED or OLIVE OIL

2 tablespoons • SESAME OIL

¼ cup or less • TERIYAKI SAUCE, good quality

• GARLIC SALT & PEPPER

Cook brown rice and put aside.

In 4 tablespoons of grape seed oil or olive oil, sauté all of the cabbage, garlic and onions. (If you want to add other veggies or meat, this would be the time.)

Now add rice and continue sautéing. Finally, add sesame oil, teriyaki sauce, garlic salt, and pepper.

Examples of veggies and meat to add: bell pepper, broccoli, green onions, chicken, steak, mushrooms... use your imagination!

Simple Stir-fry
with Minute Brown Rice

- MINUTE BROWN RICE
- BROTH of your choice for cooking rice
- COCONUT OIL or BUTTER for frying
- ANY PROTEIN such as chicken, beef, fish, pork, even tofu or eggs
- 1 clove GARLIC, chopped fine
- ONION, chopped (amount to your liking)
- PARSLEY, chopped
- VEGETABLES of your choice cut into small pieces
- GARLIC SALT, to taste
- BALSAMIC VINEGAR, optional
- SOY SAUCE, optional

Cook the Minute Brown Rice in flavored broth of your choice.

Sauté protein in coconut oil or butter.

Sauté onion, garlic and choice of vegetables in the same manner and add to the sautéed protein.

Add a little garlic salt, balsamic vinegar, or even soy sauce.

Yum!!!!

Stir Fried Brown Rice

4 cups	• BROWN RICE, cooked
2 tablespoons	• COCONUT OIL
2 tablespoons	• BUTTER
¼ pound	• SNOW PEAS
3 cups	• BOK CHOY stems and leaves, thinly sliced
4 oz. fresh	• SHITAKE MUSHROOMS, stems removed and sliced
1 whole	• SWEET ONION
½ cup	• GREEN ONIONS, chopped
1½ tablespoons	• TOASTED SESAME OIL
2 tablespoons	• SOY SAUCE, low sodium

Examples of veggies and meat to add...

• BELL PEPPER • BROCCOLI • GREEN ONIONS
• MUSHROOMS • CHICKEN • STEAK • SHRIMP

Follow directions for 4 cups of brown rice. You can use quick brown rice if you don't have a rice maker.

In a wok or pan, sauté veggies of your choice in butter and coconut oil.

Add cooked brown rice and sauté all together until veggies are done but still crispy.

Next add the sesame oil and soy sauce. Serve with your choice of cooked meat... use your imagination!

Curried Chicken Fried Rice

4 cups	●INSTANT BROWN RICE, uncooked
2 tablespoons	●BUTTER
4 cloves	●GARLIC, finely chopped
2 tablespoons fresh	●GINGER, chopped
1 large	●SWEET ONION, chopped
3 teaspoons	●CURRY POWDER
½ teaspoon	●CHILI POWDER
½ teaspoon ground	●CORIANDER
3 tablespoons	●SOY SAUCE
3 cups	●CHICKEN, cooked & shredded
3	●SCALLIONS, chopped
4 tablespoons fresh	●CILANTRO, finely chopped
1	●LIME, cut into wedges

Cook rice ahead of time and replace the water with CHICKEN BROTH.

In a saucepan, melt butter and sauté garlic, ginger, onion, and scallion.

Add rice and stir-fry. Add chicken and spices. If you need to add moisture, add some chicken broth.

Garnish with cilantro and lime wedges.

Curry is so good for you. If you want to add more, add a little at a time.

Pesto Brown Rice
with Shrimp & Mushrooms

4 cups	●INSTANT BROWN RICE, uncooked
1 pound fresh	●LARGE SHRIMP with shells on
½ cup	●MUSHROOMS, sliced
1 whole	●SWEET ONION, chopped
3 cloves	●GARLIC, minced
2 cups (more or less)	●HOMEMADE PESTO
2 tablespoons	●BUTTER
2 to 4 tablespoons	●COCONUT OIL

Cook rice ahead of time and replace the water with CHICKEN BROTH.

In a large fry pan heat up butter and coconut oil. Add onion and garlic and sauté until translucent. Add mushrooms and sauté along with garlic and onions for a few minutes. Add rice and stir fry for about 5 minutes.

Place the stir fry rice in a bowl and heat pan again. Add more butter and coconut oil. Place all of the shrimp in the pan and cook quickly on both sides. Don't overcook the shrimp and turn only once.

Add all the stir fry rice mixture and stir fry all together for a few minutes.

Add pesto and heat for a few more minutes.

Garlic Pasta

8 cups ●BARRILLA PLUS PASTA of your choice
½ cup ●WHITE WINE
5 cloves ●GARLIC, minced
¼ cup ●OLIVE OIL
¼ cup ●FRESH BASIL, chopped
1 plump ●TOMATO, chopped
●GARLIC SALT & PEPPE to taste.

After cooking pasta of your choice, drain and set aside.

In a bowl, combine rest of the ingredients. Combine pasta with rest of ingredients and gently toss.

Serve with a green salad and veggies... *oh yum!*

Pesto Pasta

1 box Barilla Plus ● ANGEL HAIR PASTA (multi-grain pasta)
1 cup ● HOMEMADE BASIL PESTO
● SALT
Freshly ground ● BLACK PEPPER to taste

Bring a large pot of lightly salted water to a boil. Add pasta, cook until al dente and drain.

Add pesto to pasta—the amount can vary, depending on your taste. Mix gently.

Salt and pepper to taste.

Delicious Pinto Beans

6 ¼ c	•WATER
1 c	•CHICKEN BROTH, condensed
2 pound	•PINTO BEANS, dried
5 cloves	•GARLIC, chopped
½	•RED ONION, chopped
5 tablespoons, or to taste	•SALT
2 tablespoons, or to taste	•GROUND BLACK PEPPER,
1 tablespoon, or to taste	•RED PEPPER FLAKES (optional)
1 (8 oz) package	•MOZZARELLA CHEESE, shredded (optional)
1 (16 oz) container	•PICO DE GALLO (optional)
	•CHOPPED VEGGIES—add any other veggies to top this off

Combine water, condensed chicken broth, beans, garlic, onion, salt, pepper, and crushed red pepper flakes in a large saucepan. Cover and bring to a simmer.

Cook, stirring occasionally, until beans are soft (about 3½ hours). You may need to add additional water to keep the beans from drying out.

Mash cooked beans with a potato masher to desired consistency.

Top with mozzarella and Pico de Gallo before serving.

Use these delicious pinto beans for tacos or for any recipe that you might use canned beans in!

Tomato Basil Mac & Cheese

1 box	•BARILLA PLUS PENNE PASTA
¼ Cup	•BUTTER
4 to 5 cups	•CHEDDAR CHEESE
½ cup	•GREEK YOGURT
1 handful	•PARMESAN CHEESE
	•GARLIC SALT, to taste
1 large	•TOMATO, chopped
1 large handful	•FRESH BASIL

Cook pasta, drain and return to pot.

Add ¼ cup butter to keep from sticking, and all of the remaining ingredients. Stir until cheese melts—sometimes you have to use little milk!

You also can turn this into a baked mac & cheese by pouring into a baking dish that is sprayed with coconut oil spray. Add additional cheese to the top and bake on 350° for 20 minutes. *Yum!*

Homemade Mashed Potatoes

4 pounds ●RED POTATOES
½ cup real ●BUTTER
2 cups ●GREEK YOGURT, plain (whole or non-fat)
●SALT & PEPPER

Place potato cubes in a pot, cover with water and boil until soft, but not falling apart.

Drain potatoes, add yogurt and butter and mash well. Be careful not to over mash because red potatoes contain a lot of gluten and will become sticky.

Add salt and pepper to taste.

My notes...

My notes...

Sweets

No Bake
Missouri Cookies

2 cups	●BROWN SUGAR
3 tablespoons	●COCOA
½ cup	●BUTTER
½ cup	●MILK
Pinch	●SALT
3 cups	●QUICK-COOKING OATS, uncooked
½ cup	●CRUNCHY PEANUT BUTTER
1 tablespoon	●VANILLA

Mix sugar, cocoa, butter, milk and salt in a saucepan. Cook to a rolling boil and continue cooking for one minute.

Remove from heat; whisk in peanut butter, and vanilla until well blended. Stir in oatmeal.

Drop by spoonful on waxed paper. Let cool until firm.

Honey Caramel Corn

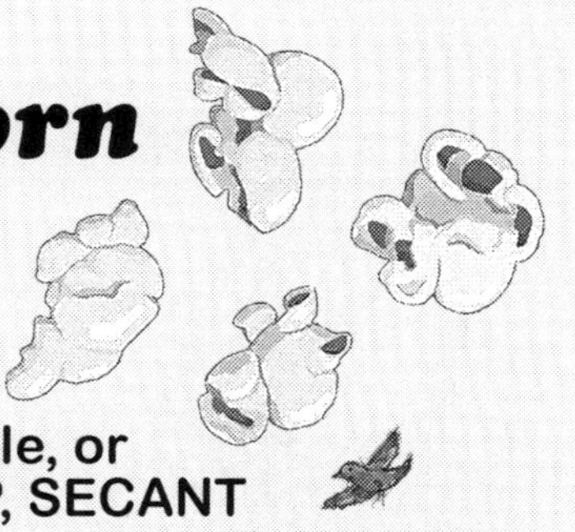

1 cup un-popped	•POPCORN, organic
⅓ cup	•COCONUT OIL
¼ – ⅓ cup	•HONEY, raw and local if possible, or you can use MAPLE SYRUP, SECANT or PALM SUGAR
¼ cup	•UNSALTED BUTTER
A few pinches	•SEA SALT, to taste

Put the popcorn and coconut oil in a large stock pot. Turn the heat up to high and put the lid on. After a few minutes, the popcorn will stop popping. Listen closely and when the pops slow down, remove the pot from the heat.

Act quickly and pour the popped popcorn into a large bowl (you might need two bowls). If you leave it in the stock pot, the popcorn at the bottom will get burned.

Put the stock pot on low heat and add the honey and butter. Stir until blended and completely melted.

Pour the butter/honey blend on the popped popcorn. Toss in a few pinches of sea salt and mix it all together until everything is well-incorporated.

If you have trouble getting it mixed together in the bowls, you can put it back into the stock pot to mix it. Serve in bowls.

Quick Fudge

1 cup	●CHOCOLATE CHIPS
¾ cup	●MINI MARSHMALLOWS
1 teaspoon	●BUTTER

Place all ingredients in a microwaveable mug or bowl and heat in microwave for approximately 1 minute. Or, if you are glamping/camping—in a pan over the fire.

Stir fast and eat hot with a spoon, or pour into a waxed paper lined pan and let cool.

You can make more fudge by doubling or tripling the recipe.

Yum!

5-minute
Strawberry Tortilla Pie

2 cups	●CHOCOLATE CHIPS, melted
6 cups	●STRAWBERRIES, washed and sliced
3 cups	●WHIPPED CREAM
6 - 10" or larger	●WHOLE WHEAT TORTILLAS

Over a burner, heat a large pan with coconut oil and fry tortillas.

On a platter, cover three cooled, crisp tortillas with strawberries.

Melt chocolate in microwave and drizzle on the strawberries.

Top with whipped cream, layering it twice, and serve garnished with a whole strawberry.

My notes...

Beverages

Peach Iced Tea

Make a pitcher of Black Tea. Let cool, pour over ICE, and add PEACH SYRUP.

If using unsweetened peach syrup, use STEVIA to sweeten the tea.

Sun Tea

Fill a clear glass jar with WATER and TEA BAGS—one tea bag per cup of water. Place in a sunny spot to steep until desired color is attained (3-8 hours).

Refrigerate to keep for a refreshing drink. When ready to enjoy, add items such as FRUITS, MINT, SYRUPS, or SWEETENER.

Flavored Iced Tea

Make your tea base using either BLACK or GREEN TEA. Add fresh fruit or use your favorite FRUIT FLAVORED SYRUP.

My notes...

My notes...

Index

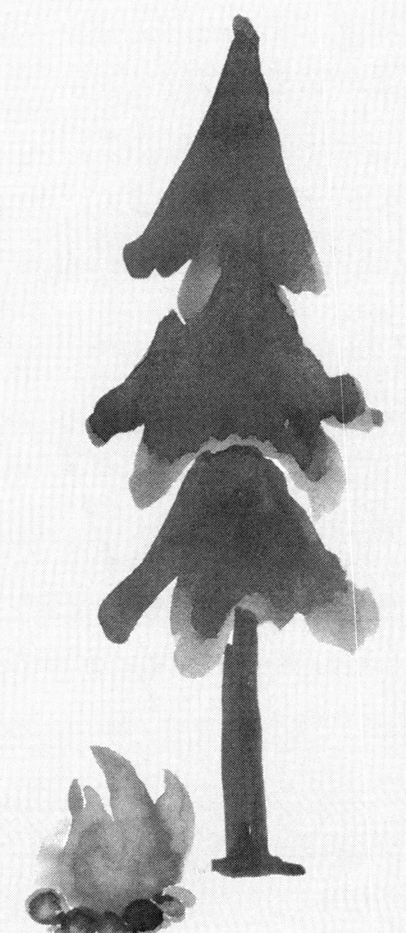

SALADS & DRESSINGS, 57

SANDWICHES & PIZZA, 31

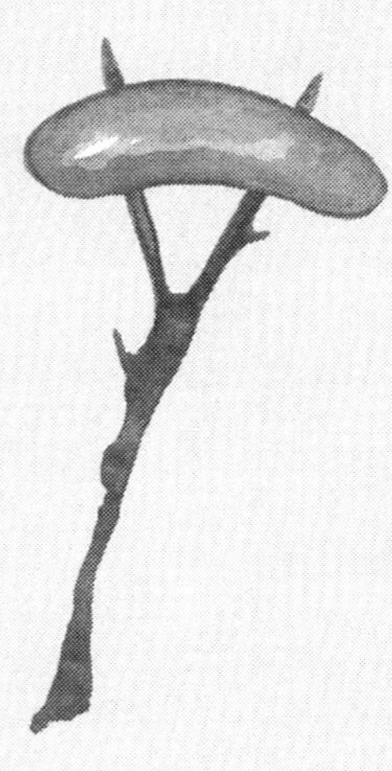

SOUPS, 17

SEAFOOD, 83

SIDE DISHES, 107

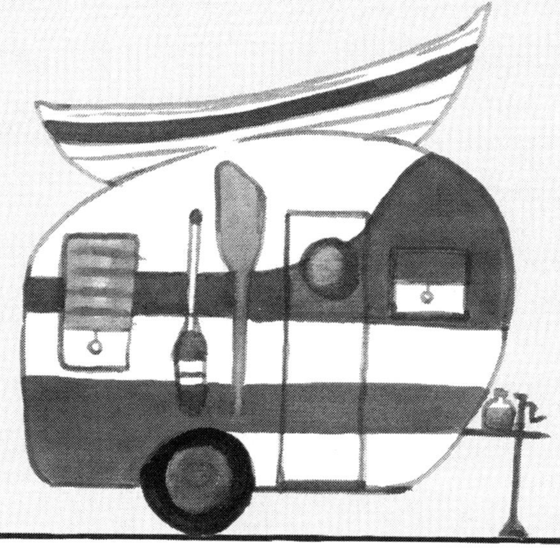

Made in the USA
Middletown, DE
13 September 2022